# THE LOVE POEMS OF
# D. H. LAWRENCE

Roy Booth lectures on D. H. Lawrence and on the literature of the English Renaissance in the English Department at Royal Holloway, University of London.

*The cover illustration* is An Idyll, by Maurice Greiffenhagen, R. A. (Walker Art Gallery, Liverpool). Lawrence began one of his four copies of this painting on the night his mother died.

*Other poetry titles published by Kyle Cathie*

*W. B. Yeats – The Love Poems*
edited by A. Norman Jeffares

*Rudyard Kipling – The Complete Verse*
introduced by M. M. Kaye

*The Selected Poems of Jonathan Swift*
edited by A. Norman Jeffares

*Joycechoyce – The Poems in Verse and Prose of James Joyce*
edited by Brendan Kennelly and A. Norman Jeffares

*The Things that Matter – An Anthology of Women's Spiritual
Poetry*
introduced by Julia Neuberger

# THE
# LOVE POEMS
# OF
# D. H. LAWRENCE

Edited with an introduction and notes by
ROY BOOTH

KYLE CATHIE LIMITED

Published in Great Britain 1993 by
Kyle Cathie Limited
3 Vincent Square
London SW1P 2LX

ISBN 1-85626-081-X

Typeset by DP Photosetting, Aylesbury, Bucks
Printed in England by Clays Ltd, St Ives plc

# CONTENTS

# THE VIRGIN MOTHER

# FROM LOOK! WE HAVE COME THROUGH!

# THE WORK OF CREATION

# LYRICS, PROFFERED WISDOMS AND SATIRES

# THE DARK DOORS

# ACKNOWLEDGEMENTS

To Laurence Pollinger Ltd and to the Estate of Frieda Lawrence Ravagli for permission to publish 'After School', 'Pear-Blossom', 'Maiden's Prayer', 'Swing Song of a Girl and a Soldier', 'The Jewess and the V.C.', a quatrain from *Mr Noon*, 'The Young Soldier with Bloody Spurs', two unpublished stanzas of 'Gipsy', an unpublished stanza of 'The Virgin Mother' and Frieda Lawrence's annotations on that poem. To the same for permission to quote from Mr. Noon. To Cambridge University Press for permission to quote from their edition of Lawrence's letters. To Francis O. Mattson of the New York Public Library, Cathy Henderson of the Harry Ransom Humanities Research Centre (University of Texas at Austin), and Betsy Bishop at the University of Chicago Library for assistance with texts; Mr David Ward of Royal Holloway, University of London, for his assistance in locating editions; the staff at the Sterling Library, University of London, Senate House; Elizabeth James at the National Art Library; to Professor A. Norman Jeffares and Mr Warwick Gould for example and inspiration. Throughout the annotation to this volume, the scholarship of the editors of the Cambridge *Letters of D. H. Lawrence*, of Keith Sagar's *D. H. Lawrence: A calendar of his work*, and especially of John Worthen's *D. H. Lawrence: The Early Years* has been my guide. To my grandfather, Mr Harry Handforth (1904–), a farmer's boy at Summerley farm, miner at the Mackerel Colliery, Unstone, and fitter at Stanton and Staveley Iron Works, a small return for his pride in me.

# INTRODUCTION

This volume brings together more than a hundred of D. H. Lawrence's poems. The basis of the selection, love poems, removes *Birds, Beasts and Flowers* from the centrality it has had in the general awareness of D. H. Lawrence as a poet (though poems from that collection are still selected here, as dealing with manifestations of desire). Instead, *Look! We Have Come Through!*, the work about which the author was 'most passionately and bitterly tender' when it came to sending it off to the press (*Letters* III, p. 94), is here the essential confrontation – Lawrence writing about the great epoch in his emotional development, how his relationship with Frieda began and became a marriage. *Look!* is therefore given a separate section here, while the rest of the poems are arranged in sections which are thematic, chronological or generic. Important among them are the love poems written during Lawrence's earlier relationships, and the poems of love and loss he wrote about his mother.

Among the eight books of poetry Lawrence published (apart from the elaborate *Collected Poems* of 1928), the first two titles, *Love Poems and Others* and *Amores*, show that Lawrence began as a poet of love. The third, *Look! We Have Come Through!* was his most deliberated effort at 'love' poetry, and was clearly considered by him to be one of his major artistic and personal projects. But even Lawrence's least successful prose fictions are more often read by students than the whole sequence, and readers of the poetry are more conversant with the poems about Lawrence and the bat or the mosquito than with his account of his contest with Frieda. While *Look! We Have Come Through!* has had its fervent advocates, it is a collection from which it is easy to discard, and, with a few exceptions, hard to select.

Lawrence twice tried to handle this particular autobiographical material. The other attempt was his unfinished and unpublished *Mr Noon*, re-approaching the theme in 1920–1 with the same narrative of 'coming through' on a journey which is both geographical (coming through the Alps, from Germany through Austria to Italy) and emotional (a travail equally arduous as both partners break free from their past lives to a new life together). *Mr Noon*, in contrast with the impassioned *Look!*, tried to deal with the events as light comedy or candid travelogue. It is regrettable, perhaps revealing, that Lawrence could not bring together the qualities which can be found in both works; and, splendid though the extremes can be – for example, Frieda's nakedness as either 'Gloire de Dijon' roses in *Look*'s lyric celebration or as 'that exquisite *finale* of Salome showing round and white behind the curtain' in *Mr Noon*'s comedy – it is possible to imagine a more self-amused *Look!* and a more engaged *Mr Noon*. The quatrain ([Unfortunate Interrupted Lovers], p. 110) retrieved here from *Mr Noon* captures the stylistic differences.

Like all of Lawrence's major works, *Look!* dared to run a risk. The poems have given readers a sense of intrusion, a sense of embarrassment that he was not embarrassed. Catherine Carswell dissuaded Lawrence from including with the poems one of the love letters he had sent to Frieda. It would have been a typical gesture, the love letter being in a genre where the writer believes unconditionally in his or her message, and where any other judgement is irrelevant. The poems, setting aside the possibility of hostility to the raptures of an adulterous eloper, are of the same nature. An understandable if glib reaction is caught in Bertrand Russell's remark, 'They may have come through but I don't see why I should look.' Aldous Huxley's 'Reading these poems was like opening the wrong bedroom door' and W. H. Auden's 'They make me feel like a peeping Tom' make the same point. Reasons for these reactions lie not simply in the poems themselves, but are more broadly cultural, and, as we all share them in part, make *Look! We Have Come Through!* an interesting challenge. English literature has had more variations on the Penitential Psalms than men confident enough to offer their own Song of Songs.

In this central expression of Lawrence as love poet, he deals with his feelings of being with his beloved in a way that is not really conventional for 'love poetry'. In this poetry, no 'I' addresses a distant 'you' in the tones of one fated to despair; persuasion, adoration and self-unworthiness are absent. Indeed, only when the situation is highly unconventional, in the love poems addressed to his mother (in the third section here, but also within the *Look!* sequence), is there an approximation in Lawrence to the hushed reverence of the courtly-poetic lover. The poetry he wrote as lover rather than son tends to be written from within a relationship, so the central theme is not unreciprocated love but the problems of mutual commitment, of how two individuals can be fulfilled within the partnership. Sex is not the unthinkable hope, but candidly present, either as failure or success; the intimacy of the poems is not rendered in observed detail, as in the poetry of the adoring eye, but in the felicity of shared response to the same experiences, the weight of body touching body, or in a record of things said.

Certain sub-genres of love poetry did assist Lawrence. He repeatedly wrote *aubades*, though his lovers do not wake together to lament the separation which the arrival of day makes inevitable, but as a married couple on honeymoon about to start daily life together. Lawrence felt impelled to write a series of rose poems, partly because poets had always done so, but most probably due to the immediate influence of W. B. Yeats. We know that he read Yeats' poetry, in part because of Frieda's admiration for it. However he produces not a sublimated rose-worship, but a poetry which tries to give voice to enjoyment and satisfaction – see, for example, 'I am Like a Rose' and 'The Rose of all the World' opposite Yeats' 'The Rose of the World' and others in *W. B. Yeats, The Love Poems* (ed. A. Norman Jeffares, Kyle Cathie Ltd, 1990).

The general acceptance within literary taste of a poetry enacting yearning at a distance is no surprise. The act of reading is closer to the experience of solitary desire than that of shared delight. Perhaps John Donne did most with a poetry of mutual delight, but he gave it sympathetic appeal with a charge of nervous energy from illicitness and distrust, from the alarming conceits in which total eclipse follows rapidly upon the zenith of love.

Lawrence measured his own distance from a preferred literary tradition in the pamphlet *Pornography and Obscenity* (1929), where he cites and comments upon a remark made by a critic:

'If Mr Lawrence's attitude to sex were adopted, then two things would disappear, the love-lyric and the smoking room story.' And this, I think, is true. But it depends on which love-lyrics he means. If it is the 'Who is Sylvia what is she?' – then it may just as well disappear. All that pure and heaven-blessed stuff is only the counterpart to the smoking room story. . . . But if it is a question of the sound love-lyric, My love is like a red, red rose – ! then we are on other ground.

He uses the Burns poem, which is about possessing love, as a positive of erotic poetry, while the Elizabethan lyric, adulating a Sylvia who is scarcely known for herself at all, is associated, in this post-*Chatterley* pamphlet, with a dirty story. Lawrence perhaps remembered that this song is performed by the mobile-hearted Proteus, as if the male adorer easily mutates into a man who tells offensive jokes about the same woman. When Lawrence wrote in a consciously 'Elizabethan' way in the poem 'Sigh No More', it was as a means to accommodate uncomfortable feelings about his own insincerity ('Sigh no more, Ladies, . . . Men were deceivers ever' goes the Shakespearean original). In the end, Clifford Chatterley would be characterised by a taste for Elizabethan poetry, which betrays his emotional pettiness and chilly nature.

But while he could approve of Burns, Lawrence wanted to go beyond a poetry that simply celebrated physical fulfilment. He tried to write a type of love poetry that barely exists in his cultural tradition, a poetry of what *Mr Noon* calls (in characteristic extreme idiom) 'true, terrible, marriage'. The contemplated alternative titles for *Look! We Have Come Through!* included 'Poems of a Married Man'. Any anthology of the poetry of connubial love, a relatively rare subject, would include a high proportion of failed applications to the Muse. Spenser, who, like Lawrence, wrote his own Epithalamion (marriage-song), was nevertheless constrained and circumspect. His sonnets, *Amoretti*, preserve much of the decorum of Petrarchan adoration. The eccentric mutual effusions of the Duke and Duchess of Newcastle, and some of the more gushing parts of the Victorian canon (both Brownings, Tennyson, Patmore), barely sustain a type of writing which finally dips away from formal literary pretentions into privately published wedding anniversary messages, birthday odes of gratitude and home-made newspaper epitaphs (the best matrimonial love poetry has always been elegiac).

It really does require Mozart's music to make 'Mann und Weib, und Weib und Mann' a sublime affirmation.

Lawrence wanted to create great art out of the forging of marriage, to be a Rembrandt. He felt fervently about the sacredness of marriage. *Mr Noon* (chapter 18) has an authorial polemic about the necessity of marriage to passion ('Only those who know one another in the intricate dark ways of physical custom can pass through the seven dark hells and the seven bright heavens of sensual fulfilment'), and the suggestion here of entry into a freemasonry of heterosexual initiants recalls the hieratic formalisations of the poem 'Paradise Re-entered'.

*Look!* actually comes closest to fulfilling Lawrence's aims when his attention is half distracted by the beauty of the outer world or richness of the intimate setting, and is at its worst when he is asserting his truths in pieces like 'Manifesto'. At best, the poems have the effect of taking one of the stiff, squinting, black and white photographs of Lawrence and Frieda, and flooding it with colour, adding voices. The magic of abroad (it was, after all, Lawrence's first trip overseas, though he was instantly and lastingly attuned to travel) and of love found at last in an uncustomary landscape fills the sequence. Lawrence needed to travel, his hunger for symbolic experiences impelled him: look how definitively 'Lawrentian' a moment 'Sunday Morning in Italy' records.

The publication of *Look! We Have Come Through!* in 1917 represented an extraordinary feat of self-severance from the world. Against a background of disastrous war, Lawrence issued a celebration of personal victory. A touch of retrospective unease perhaps appears in the 1928 preface to his *Collected Poems:* 'One would like to ask the reader of *Look! We Have Come Through!* to fill in the background of the poems, as far as possible, with the place, the time, the circumstance. What was uttered in the cruel spring of 1917 should not be dislocated and heard as if sounding out of the void.' The request hardly seems legitimate, and that it is made at all reveals much about the sublime nescience of the sequence Lawrence revised for publication through January and February 1917. There is always a bit more to forgive with Lawrence, who didn't attempt a separation of his experience into the personal and the literary, who was ready to rejoice while a humbled Europe wept, and who had no notion that mutual pleasure and displeasure were unsuitable subjects. He can be considered English literature's amazing crossed telephone line or unignorable neighbour, an all too audible voice raised in ecstasy or disagreement: just listen what they are saying to one another!

The poems of *Look! We Have Come Through!* show Lawrence's verse in a transitional state, between the sometimes studied literariness of the poems from his Croydon years, and the idiosyncratic improvisations of the animal and flower poems. The poem 'Bei Hennef' has been identified by Sandra Gilbert as the formative compositional experience: Lawrence wrote these words while he waited for a train, and to have revised them would have been to sacrifice their authenticating spontaneity. The poem can be used to comment on itself:

> *You are the call and I am the answer,*
> *You are the wish, and I the fulfilment,*
> *You are the night, and I the day.*
> *What else? it is perfect enough.*

where the 'it' in the last quoted line is the moment and relationship the poem describes, but also the poem itself, the faintly self-contradictory 'perfect enough' a defiance to the idea of formal correctness. The poem is so purely an utterance of that moment that to revise its absolute statements would be to vitiate the relationship which produced it, sacrificing essential truth to literary taste.

Despite the recalcitrant theme Lawrence chose, and a poetic art which sometimes falls between formal and free verse, this selection hopes to redirect some attention to *Look!*, which through all its stumblings and unease is driven and made vital by hope and belief in love.

The opening three sections here present Lawrence through poems written before this central collection.

The 'Early Love Poems' are largely taken from *Love Poems and Others* and *Amores*. Readers familiar with Lawrence's novels will recognise some close correspondences with *The White Peacock* and *Sons and Lovers*. My notes to the poems indicate the main parallels. Lawrence

> thought [*Love Poems and Others*] awfully nice – I loved it. F[rieda] refuses to have sufficient respect for it – but there, she **would**. There are too many heroines other than herself.' (*Letters* I: 462)

The central 'heroines' were Jessie Chambers, Helen Corke and Louie Burrows; other pieces selected here are more fictional in nature. Much of the love poetry Lawrence was writing at this time was, to be frank, manipulative, used in emotional tests and in semi-declarations of desire. His game seems to have been known well enough for Willie Hopkin to allege that Lawrence used as an entrance-line into Alice Dax's house, 'There's a poem I want to write,' followed by, 'I can never work until after I've had sexual intercourse,' in order to seduce her. Jessie Chambers more reliably records how Lawrence's early sense of himself as 'poet', passionate but safe sexually, conflicted with a desire, like that of W. B. Yeats, to 'call to my own opposite':

> He felt himself a medium charged with some power for the good of mankind. Yet he wished he could escape it and grow stout, and attractive to women. He longed to be loved as a man instead of as a poet.

From the insight provided by the early poems, we can see how imperative it was for Lawrence to become Frieda's poet and *Look! We Have Come Through!* as the work which truly united these two selves. But the early poetic posture was always ambiguous, partly through the potentialities Willie Hopkin crudely caricatured, and also because this poetry has a coercive aspect. There is a relish for erotic cruelty in poems like 'Love on the Farm' which is, finally, all too like his dismaying treatment of Jessie Chambers.

The section 'The Virgin Mother' shows Lawrence at his most worshipping, in poems which recurrently address their subject as 'love' or 'darling', and here the true Petrarchan note of self-consecration to the memory of the dear departed appears. These are, as Graham Hough has said, 'Straightforward poem[s] of personal love ... too directly felt and expressed to be other than moving' (*Hough*, p. 201). After *Sons and Lovers*, nothing much need be added from Lawrence on the love he had for his mother and its effects in halting his emotional growth. Jessie Chambers gives understated but effective witness: 'Lawrence was loath to admit that boyhood was over. He was most reluctant to begin shaving,' or 'He turned for home like a man in a trance of love. This happened a week or so before his twentieth birthday.'

Myth-based readings of Lawrence's poems have seen his mother in his recurrent use of the Persephone story, the girl abducted by the terrible bridegroom. But Lawrence was not a Tennyson, seeking the consoling power in the literary myths of loss and restoration. The older poetic voice which presses into these poems is that of ballad poetry, which is the poetry of drastic terminations, of the inescapable claims made by the dead on the living, of burials, mourning, wild grief and, it might be added, incestuous love. The slow and terrible revelation of why his love is 'uncanny cold' in 'The Bride', the 'strange countrie' of 'The Virgin Mother' and the hopeless 'But never . . . and never' of 'Everlasting Flowers' are effects recollected from the traditional ballad. It is perhaps a similar kind of connectedness with unsophisticated sentiment which gives Lawrence, a product of the Congregational Chapel, his passionate recognition of a need met in the Italian Giorno dei Morti ceremonies:

> *Naked candles burn on every grave.*
> *On your grave, in England, the weeds grow.*
> *('All Souls')*

In grief, as in his love poetry, Lawrence found little in polite literature to help express feelings as vehement as his own, and produced something equally challenging to the English tradition.

Lawrence knew enough about ballad poetry to accomplish a series of narratives in dialect. 'Violets' is a tale of graveside desperation, a fairly standard literary ballad Hardy or Emily Brontë might have produced, though in revision it seems to have taken on the weather experienced at the burial of Lawrence's mother. 'Whether or Not' and 'The Drained Cup' revisit the ballads of seduction, the dire combat of the sexes, and are more Lawrentian, especially 'Whether or Not' as re-worked for the 1928 *Collected Poems*, which is the version given here. Lawrence had written these poems around September 1911 at the instigation of Edward Garnett. As Worthen perceptively remarks, 'This was the kind of work people expected from the son of a coal-miner' (*Worthen*, p. 217). In 'Whether or Not', the 'or Not' ending, where Tim declares he will not marry Lizzie, was added after Lawrence had some experience with similar decisions in his own life, at the expense of Louie Burrows and Jessie Chambers. Personal experience creeps into even these most apparently fictional poems. 'The Drained Cup' is one of Lawrence's poems voiced for a woman speaker (like 'Love on the Farm', 'Wedding Morn', etc.). Unsurprisingly for the author of *The Rainbow* and *Women in Love*, these are among his most powerful poems.

The final narrative poem in section two is 'The Young Soldier with Bloody Spurs'. This, like the early 'Love on the Farm' and the scene with Gerald and his mare at the railway crossing in *Women in Love*, uses cruelty to an animal to suggest mastery and cruelty in love. Without dialect, the poem is less striking, but the student of Lawrence might like to look at the prose re-telling of the same incident in *Mr Noon* (chapter 19), where the Servant Girl who speaks the poem, the story of her seduction, is replaced by Gilbert Noon, Lawrence's thin fictionalisation of himself. Gilbert's fascination with the cruelly masculine soldier is part of the greater frankness about homosexual feelings which marks Lawrence's fiction. However, he was not able to write a poem about his homosexual impulses or love: 'Snake' comes closest, but is a poem of fascination and revulsion. It is included in this selection of the love poetry as a poem with a conspicuous sexual sub-text.

The potent male figures of the novels are largely absent from the poems. Gamekeepers and miners, guardian spirits of the woods and voyagers into the underworld, so powerfully present in the fiction, will be sought in vain. Lawrence himself is the leading man, the action is heterosexual, and any homoeroticism narcissistic. There is only the faintly funny policeman Tim of 'Whether or Not'. It might be added that Lawrence wrote little poetry about his father. The verses 'Discord in Childhood', a poem of hate rather than love, stands for that absence.

But to confine a selection of Lawrence's love poetry to his poems about human relationships would be impoverishing and unrepresentative. Lawrence had an impassioned life-long love affair with flowers – the intensity of feeling they provoked in him deserves that description (see, for substantiation, the footnote on 'Bavarian Gentians', p. 155) – and a series of shorter, intense dealings with animals. His uncanny imaginative sympathy sometimes flashes across the species barrier – he becomes the pursuing stag ('A Doe at Evening'), or lioness's mate, or he expresses the sex instinct of an ass or a tortoise. If he projects human feeling on to the animals, it was with the general awareness that 'anthropomorphism is a bore. Too much anthropos makes the world a dull hole' (quoted from 'Him with his Tail in his Mouth'); much of the Lawrentian doctrine was aiming at the reverse process, to make sex a matter of attuned instinct and less tainted by the mind. The fifth section draws together some of the best of Lawrence's soundings on what can be known about desire from the non-human.

'Mountain Lion' is Lawrence's strangest love poem, perhaps his best. The opening of the poem is on a 'vanishing trail' at the very threshold between one state and another, the moment for Lawrence's most awakened attention. After his encounter with the emerging hunters, he enters the 'dark and snow and inwardness of the Lobo valley', and, already in love with the lioness after the caressive lines on the animal's face – which seem like variations on Webster's celebrated 'Cover her face: mine eyes dazzle. She died young' – painstakingly installs himself in her lair as a bereaved mate: 'And I think in this empty world there was room for me and a mountain lion'. He thinks the ferocious lion thoughts of the close 'And I think in the world beyond, how easily we might spare a million or two of humans/And never miss them'.

That is one way to account for the opinion expressed at the end of the poem, but there are moments when Lawrence lets slip the same sentiment without there being any sense of special identification with the ferocious (see, in *Complete Poems*, 'Humanity needs pruning' or 'There are too many people'). Lawrence's genius operated very close to the self-indulgent modes of loose talk, as in the audacious laziness of 'Peach'. The outburst of hatred which ends this fascinating poem might be accepted as part of its challenge. Teachers struggling with classes who brazenly agree with the poem's ending might like to note that the inevitable ecological argument much post-dates the poem: the Lawrences came back from Mexico happy to exhibit a snow-leopard skin as a souvenir.

Lawrence was impelled to improvise an ideology to justify each and all of his personal prejudices, whether it was a preference for free verse over formal verse, or in his attitudes towards mountain lionesses, women, forms of society and types of sex. The section, 'Lyrics, Proffered Wisdoms and Satires' includes selections from *Pansies* (his 'pensees'), and while the general principle of selection – love poetry – hardly admits Lawrence at his most cantankerous, there should be poems here to argue over or feel guilty about agreeing with. Though

Lawrence could be arbitrary and impossible, there always remain the moments of self-deflating common sense, as well as the veracities. *Pansies* are the minor poems Lawrence composed in 1928–9 at Bandol. Graham Hough (in *The Dark Sun*) brilliantly characterises them as 'epigrammatic precipitations of ideas that are floating about in all Lawrence's later work'. The image of the desperately ill Lawrence, sitting up in bed, wearing a straw hat, sunnily firing off these squibs, his 'rag poems' as Catherine Carswell said he called them, or laughing and reading them out as they came, is a fine image of the great life artist: 'Being able to express one's soul keeps one alive' (quoted from Lawrence's 'Getting On', *Worthen*, p. 326).

The final section, 'The Dark Doors', continues from *Pansies* into Lawrence's last poems. This section is meant to be cathartic, after all the hectic ardours and protean imagination of the prior sections. These are poems about the dying of desire, leading into the poems about the desire of dying. Frieda says that Lawrence was impotent in his last years. In the final months of his life, she was forbidden entry to his bedroom until after dawn, when his first and worst fit of coughing and haemorrhage was over. There was no 'last poem' penned immediately before dying: Lawrence wrote no poetry after December 1929, but there are among his last compositions several that might be chosen as a final statement. Instead of the frequently anthologised 'Shadows', which seems more prayer than poem, I have decided to close the volume with 'All Souls' Day', for its dignified and impersonal revisit to the day of celebration of the dead which had previously produced the hysterical self-dedication to his mother's memory expressed in 'All Souls'. The unhaunted poem shows his hard-earned peace.

To return, in conclusion, to the main claim for a redirection of attention this collection makes, these love poems were written for a series of 'heroines'. Frieda was the most important, perhaps because she believed least in Lawrence as poet. Frieda had reason to hesitate, as she was being versified so directly: 'Then would he write poems for me, poems I took a little anxiously, seeing he knew me so well.' Her robust opinion emerges via jest: when Lawrence sailed dangerously in the sea off Lerici where Shelley had drowned, Frieda yelled, 'If you can't be a real poet, you'll drown like one, anyhow.' The *Pansies* were, in her opinion, 'real doggerel'. She made him into a notable twentieth-century poet by her personal and aesthetic resistance. *Look! We Have Come Through!* can be seen as the manageable dialogue, the enacting of uninterrupted communion, the luxury of uncontradicted statement, even as dressings for the psychic wounds she inflicted. Her antagonistic collaboration severed Lawrence from the mode of 'Poetry of the Past', freed his demon. Lawrence wrote the words, but Frieda dictated the experience: *we* have come through.

# ABOUT THE TEXTS CHOSEN

If an 'Oxford Book of Spontaneous Verse' was put together, D. H. Lawrence would be its Alexander Pope. His belief in a poetry of the immediate present went hand in hand with being a careful reworker, reviser and re-arranger of his impromptus. He was never trying to create an artful impression of spontaneity, revision for Lawrence was a matter of getting closer to what had escaped in the first composition. In the preface to his *Collected Poems* in 1928, he explained: 'A young man is afraid of his demon and puts his hand over the demon's mouth sometimes and speaks for him. And the things the young man says are very rarely poetry. So I have tried to let the demon have his say, and to remove the passages where the young man intruded.' The notes to this volume only present earlier variants where they seem especially revealing. The source of the text is indicated, and generally for the early poems it is Lawrence's revision for *Collected Poems*. Keith Sagar's arguments (see notes on these poems) about 'Bavarian Gentians' and 'The Ship of Death' have been accepted here, and those poems are therefore presented in their less familiar revised texts.

# EARLY LOVE POEMS

The poems in this section were first written between 1907, when Lawrence was twenty-two, and early 1912. They mainly concern his involvements with Jessie Chambers, Helen Corke, and his fiancée Louie Burrows.

# Cherry Robbers

Under the long dark boughs, like jewels red
   In the hair of an Eastern girl
Hang strings of crimson cherries, as if had bled
   Blood-drops beneath each curl.

Under the glistening cherries, with folded wings
   Three dead birds lie:
Pale-breasted throstles and a blackbird, robberlings
   Stained with red dye.

Against the haystack a girl stands laughing at me,
   Cherries hung round her ears.
Offers me her scarlet fruit: I will see
   If she has any tears.

# After School

In a little, half-built street, where red and white villas
Look brightly on a confusion of mud, and sand, and mortar,
As I came home in the dusk, despoiled by school, a mere blossomless
   husk—
A light like mellow moonlight gleamed on the water
In the deep cart-ruts, gleamed through the blue of the darkening
   dusk,
And I looked in a room where the lamp, as a moon in mist
Shone sweetly through yellow silk: a man full in the light,
Looked up, and the words moved like a smile from his lips.
A woman came into the glow from out of the shadowy light
Leans over to read his work, and her dark head dips
Deep into the heart of the light, the centre of a star,
There in the heart of a star set far off in the night
She turned and kissed him, and his eyes were the soul of the star,
And the white nape of her neck was the beauty of the star
And I, in immeasurable night, looked on from afar,—afar!

# Wedding Morn

The morning breaks like a pomegranate
   In a shining crack of red;
Ah, when to-morrow the dawn comes late
   Whitening across the bed
It will find me watching at the marriage gate
   And waiting while light is shed
On him who is sleeping satiate
   With a sunk, unconscious head.

And when the dawn comes creeping in,
   Cautiously I shall raise
Myself to watch the daylight win
   On my first of days,
As it shows him sleeping a sleep he got
   With me, as under my gaze
He grows distinct, and I see his hot
   Face freed of the wavering blaze.

Then I shall know which image of God
   My man is made toward;
And I shall see my sleeping rod
   Or my life's reward;
And I shall count the stamp and worth
   Of the man I've accepted as mine,
Shall see an image of heaven or of earth
   On his minted metal shine.

Oh, and I long to see him sleep
   In my power utterly;
So I shall know what I have to keep. . . .
   I long to see
My love, that spinning coin, laid still
   And plain at the side of me
For me to reckon—for surely he will
   Be wealth of life to me.

And then he will be mine, he will lie
    Revealed to me;
Patent and open beneath my eye
    He will sleep of me;
He will lie negligent, resign
    His truth to me, and I
Shall watch the dawn light up for me
    This fate of mine.

And as I watch the wan light shine
    On his sleep that is filled of me,
On his brow where the curved wisps clot and twine
    Carelessly,
On his lips where the light breaths come and go
    Unconsciously,
On his limbs in sleep at last laid low
    Helplessly,
I shall weep, oh, I shall weep, I know
    For joy or for misery.


## Love on the Farm

What large, dark hands are those at the window
Grasping in the golden light
Which weaves its way through the evening wind
    At my heart's delight?

Ah, only the leaves! But in the west
I see a redness suddenly come
Into the evening's anxious breast—
    'Tis the wound of love goes home!

The woodbine creeps abroad
Calling low to her lover:
    The sun-lit flirt who all the day
    Has poised above her lips in play
    And stolen kisses, shallow and gay

Of pollen, now has gone away—
    She woos the moth with her sweet, low word:
And when above her his moth-wings hover
Then her bright breast she will uncover
And yield her honey-drop to her lover.

Into the yellow, evening glow
Saunters a man from the farm below;
Leans, and looks in at the low-built shed
Where the swallow has hung her marriage bed.
    The bird lies warm against the wall.
    She glances quick her startled eyes
    Towards him, then she turns away
    Her small head, making warm display
    Of red upon the throat. Her terrors sway
    Her out of the nest's warm, busy ball,
    Whose plaintive cry is heard as she flies
    In one blue stoop from out the sties
    Into the twilight's empty hall.

Oh, water-hen, beside the rushes
Hide your quaintly scarlet blushes,
Still your quick tail, lie still as dead,
Till the distance folds over his ominous tread!

The rabbit presses back her ears,
Turns back her liquid, anguished eyes
And crouches low; then with wild spring
Spurts from the terror of *his* oncoming;
To be choked back, the wire ring
Her frantic effort throttling:
    Piteous brown ball of quivering fears!
Ah, soon in his large, hard hands she dies,
And swings all loose from the swing of his walk!
Yet calm and kindly are his eyes
And ready to open in brown surprise
Should I not answer to his talk
Or should he my tears surmise.

I hear his hand on the latch, and rise from my chair
Watching the door open; he flashes bare
His strong teeth in a smile, and flashes his eyes
In a smile like triumph upon me; then careless-wise
He flings the rabbit soft on the table board
And comes towards me: ah! the uplifted sword
Of his hand against my bosom! and oh, the broad
Blade of his glance that asks me to applaud
His coming! With his hand he turns my face to him
And caresses me with his fingers that still smell grim
Of the rabbit's fur! God, I am caught in a snare!
I know not what fine wire is round my throat;
I only know I let him finger there
My pulse of life, and let him nose like a stoat
Who sniffs with joy before he drinks the blood.

And down his mouth comes to my mouth! and down
His bright dark eyes come over me, like a hood
Upon my mind! his lips meet mine, and a flood
Of sweet fire sweeps across me, so I drown
Against him, die, and find death good.

# *Aware*

Slowly the moon is rising out of the ruddy haze,
Divesting herself of her golden shift, and so
Emerging white and exquisite; and I in amaze
See in the sky before me, a woman I did not know
I loved, but there she goes, and her beauty hurts my heart;
I follow her down the night, begging her not to depart.

# Lightning

I felt the lurch and halt of her heart
    Next my breast, where my own heart was beating;
And I laughed to feel it plunge and bound,
And strange in my blood-swept ears was the sound
    Of the words I kept repeating,
Repeating with tightened arms, and the hot blood's blind-fold art.

Her breath flew warm against my neck,
    Warm as a flame in the close night air;
And the sense of her clinging flesh was sweet
Where her arms and my neck's thick pulse could meet
    Holding her thus, could I care
That the black night hid her from me, blotted out every speck?

I leaned in the darkness to find her lips
    And claim her utterly in a kiss,
When the lightning flew across her face
And I saw her for the flaring space
    Of a second, like snow that slips
From a roof, inert with death, weeping 'Not this! Not this!'

A moment there, like snow in the dark
    Her face lay pale against my breast,
Pale love lost in a thaw of fear
And melted in an icy tear,
    And open lips, distressed;
A moment; then darkness shut the lid of the sacred ark.

And I heard the thunder, and felt the rain,
    And my arms fell loose, and I was dumb.
Almost I hated her, sacrificed;
Hated myself, and the place, and the iced
    Rain that burnt on my rage; saying: Come
Home, come home, the lightning has made it too plain!

## *Lilies in the Fire (III)*

I am ashamed, you wanted me not to-night.
And it is always so, you sigh against me.
Your brightness dims when I draw too near, and my free
Fire enters you like frost, like a cruel blight.

And now I know, so I must be ashamed;
You love me while I hover tenderly
Like moonbeams kissing you; but the body of me
Closing upon you in the lightning-flamed

Moment, destroys you, you are just destroyed.
Humiliation deep to me, that all my best
Soul's naked lightning, which should sure attest
God stepping through our loins in one bright stride

Means but to you a burden of dead flesh
Heavy to bear, even heavy to uprear
Again from earth, like lilies flagged and sere
Upon the floor, that erst stood up so fresh.

## *Sigh No More*

The cuckoo and the coo-dove's ceaseless calling,
          Calling,
Of a meaningless monotony is palling
All my morning's pleasure in the sun-fleck-scattered wood.

May-blossom and blue bird's-eye flowers falling,
          Falling
In a litter through the elm-tree shade are scrawling
Messages of true-love down the dust of the highroad.

I do not like to hear the gentle grieving,
        Grieving
Of the she-dove in the blossom, still believing
Love will yet again return to her and make all good.

When I know that there must ever be deceiving,
        Deceiving
Of the mournful constant heart, that while she's weaving
Her woes, her lover woos and sings within another wood.

Oh, boisterous the cuckoo shouts, forestalling,
        Stalling
A progress down the intricate enthralling
By-paths where the wanton-headed flowers doff their hood.

And like a laughter leads me onward, heaving,
        Heaving
A sigh among the shadows, thus retrieving
A decent short regret for that which once was very good.

## Seven Seals

Since this is the last night I keep you home,
Come, I will consecrate you for the journey.

Rather I had you would not go. Nay come,
I will not again reproach you. Lie back
And let me love you a long time ere you go.
For you are sullen-hearted still, and lack
The will to love me. But even so
I will set a seal upon you from my lip,
Will set a guard of honour at each door,
Seal up each channel out of which might slip
Your love for me.

                       I kiss your mouth. Ah, love,
Could I but seal its ruddy, shining spring
Of passion, parch it up, destroy, remove
Its softly-stirring crimson welling-up
Of kisses! Oh, help me, God! Here at the source
I'd lie for ever drinking and drawing in
Your fountains, as heaven drinks from out their course
The floods.

              I close your ears with kisses
And seal your nostrils; and round your neck you'll wear—
Nay, let me work—a delicate chain of kisses.
Like beads they go around, and not one misses
To touch its fellow on either side.

                          And there
Full mid-between the champaign of your breast
I place a great and burning seal of love
Like a dark rose, a mystery of rest
On the slow bubbling of your rhythmic heart.
Nay, I persist, and very faith shall keep
You integral to me. Each door, each mystic port
Of egress from you I will seal and steep
In perfect chrism.
                 Now it is done. The mort
Will sound in heaven before it is undone.
But let me finish what I have begun
And shirt you now invulnerable in the mail
Of iron kisses, kisses linked like steel.
Put greaves upon your thighs and knees, and frail
Webbing of steel on your feet. So you shall feel
Ensheathed invulnerable with me, with seven
Great seals upon your outgoings, and woven
Chain of my mystic will wrapped perfectly
Upon you, wrapped in indomitable me.

# Last Words to Miriam

Yours is the sullen sorrow,
    The disgrace is also mine;
Your love was intense and thorough,
Mine was the love of a growing flower
    For the sunshine.

You had the power to explore me,
    Blossom me stalk by stalk;
You woke my spirit, you bore me
To consciousness, you gave me the dour
    Awareness—then I suffered a balk.

Body to body I could not
    Love you, although I would.
We kissed, we kissed though we should not.
You yielded, we threw the last cast,
    And it was no good.

You only endured, and it broke
    My craftsman's nerve.
No flesh responded to my stroke;
So I failed to give you the last
    Fine torture you did deserve.

You are shapely, you are adorned
    But opaque and null in the flesh;
Who, had I but pierced with the thorned
Full anguish, perhaps had been cast
    In a lovely illumined mesh

Like a painted window; the best
    Fire passed through your flesh,
Undrossed it, and left it blest
In clean new awareness. But now
    Who shall take you afresh?

Now who will burn you free
  From your body's deadness and dross?
Since the fire has failed in me.
What man will stoop in your flesh to plough
  The shrieking cross?

A mute, nearly beautiful thing
  Is your face, that fills me with shame
As I see it hardening;
I should have been cruel enough to bring
  You through the flame.

# The Yew-Tree on the Downs

A gibbous moon hangs out of the twilight,
  Star-spiders, spinning their thread,
Drop a little lower, withouten respite
  Watching us overhead.

Come then under this tree, where the tent-cloths
  Curtain us in so dark
That here we're safe from even the ermine moth's
  Twitching remark.

Here in this swarthy, secret tent,
  Whose black boughs flap the ground,
Come, draw the thorn from my discontent,
  And bless the wound.

This rare, ancient night! For in here
  Under the yew-tree tent
The darkness is secret, and I could sear
  You like frankincense into scent.

Here not even the stars can spy us,
  Not even the moths can alight
On our mystery; nought can descry us
  Nor put us to flight.

Put trust then now in the black-boughed tree,
  Lie down, and open to me
The inner dark of the mystery,
  Be penetrate, like the tree.

Waste not the yew-tree's waiting, waste
  Not this inner night!
Open the core of gloaming, taste
  The last dark delight.

# Kisses in the Train

I saw the midlands
  Revolve through her hair;
The fields of autumn
  Stretching bare,
And sheep on the pasture
  Tossed back in a scare.

And still as ever
  The world went round,
My mouth on her pulsing
  Throat was found,
And my breast to her beating
  Breast was bound.

But my heart at the centre
  Of all, in a swound
Was still as a pivot,
  As all the ground
On its prowling orbit
  Shifted round.

And still in my nostrils
    The scent of her flesh;
And still my blind face
    Sought her afresh;
And still one pulse
    Through the world did thresh.

And the world all whirling
    Round in joy
Like the dance of a dervish
    Did destroy
My sense—and reason
    Spun like a toy.

But firm at the centre
    My heart was found;
My own to her perfect
    Heartbeat bound,
Like a magnet's keeper
    Closing the round.


# *Snap-Dragon*

She bade me follow to her garden, where
The mellow sunlight stood as in a cup
Between the old grey walls; I did not dare
To raise my face, I did not dare look up,
Lest her bright eyes like sparrows should fly in
My windows of discovery, and shrill 'Sin!'

So with a downcast mien and laughing voice
I followed, followed the swing of her white dress
That rocked in a lilt along; I watched the poise
Of her feet as they flew for a space, then paused to press
The grass deep down with the royal burden of her;
And gladly I'd offered my breast to the tread of her.

'I like to see,' she said, and she crouched her down,
She sunk into my sight like a settling bird;
And her bosom couched in the confines of her gown
Like heavy birds at rest there, softly stirred
By her measured breaths: 'I like to see,' said she,
'The snap-dragon put out his tongue at me.'

She laughed, she reached her hand out to the flower,
Closing its crimson throat. My own throat in her power
Strangled, my heart swelled up so full
As if it would burst its wine-skin in my throat,
Choke me in my own crimson. I watched her pull
The gorge of the gaping flower, till the blood did float

    Over my eyes, and I was blind—
    Her large brown hand stretched over
    The windows of my mind;
    And there in the dark I did discover
    Things I was out to find:

My Grail, a brown bowl twined
With swollen veins that met in the wrist,
Under whose brown the amethyst
I longed to taste! I longed to turn
My heart's red measure in her cup;
I longed to feel my hot blood burn
With the amethyst in her cup.

Then suddenly she looked up,
And I was blind in a tawny-gold day.
Till she took her eyes away.

So she came down from above
And emptied my heart of love.
So I held my heart aloft
To the cuckoo that hung like a dove,
And she settled soft.

It seemed that I and the morning world
Were pressed cup-shape to take this reiver
Bird who was weary to have furled
Her wings in us,
As we were weary to receive her.

> *This bird, this rich,*
> *Sumptuous central grain;*
> *This mutable witch,*
> *This one refrain,*
> *This laugh in the fight,*
> *This clot of night,*
> *This field of delight.*

She spoke, and I closed my eyes
To shut hallucinations out.
I echoed with surprise
Hearing my mere lips shout
The answer they did devise.

> Again I saw a brown bird hover
> Over the flowers at my feet;
> I felt a brown bird hover
> Over my heart, and sweet
> Its shadow lay on my heart.
> I thought I saw on the clover
> A brown bee pulling apart
> The closed flesh of the clover
> And burrowing in its heart.

> She moved her hand, and again
> I felt the brown bird cover
> My heart; and then
> The bird came down on my heart,
> As on a nest the rover
> Cuckoo comes, and shoves over

The brim each careful part
Of love, takes possession, and settles her down,
With her wings and her feathers to drown
The nest in a heat of love.

She turned her flushed face to me for the glint
Of a moment.—'See,' she laughed, 'if you also
Can make them yawn!'—I put my hand to the dint
In the flower's throat, and the flower gaped wide with woe.
She watched, she went of a sudden intensely still,
She watched my hand, to see what it would fulfil.

I pressed the wretched, throttled flower between
My fingers, till its head lay back, its fangs
Poised at her. Like a weapon my hand was white and keen,
And I held the choked flower-serpent in its pangs
Of mordant anguish, till she ceased to laugh,
Until her pride's flag, smitten, cleaved down to the staff.

She hid her face, she murmured between her lips
The low word 'Don't'!—I let the flower fall,
But held my hand afloat towards the slips
Of blossom she fingered, and my fingers all
Put forth to her: she did not move, nor I,
For my hand like a snake watched hers, that could not fly.

Then I laughed in the dark of my heart, I did exult
Like a sudden chuckling of music. I bade her eyes
Meet mine, I opened her helpless eyes to consult
Their fear, their shame, their joy that underlies
Defeat in such a battle. In the dark of her eyes
My heart was fierce to make her laughter rise.

Till her dark deeps shook with convulsive thrills, and the dark
Of her spirit wavered like water thrilled with light;
And my heart leaped up in longing to plunge its stark
Fervour within the pool of her twilight,
Within her spacious soul, to find delight.

And I do not care, though the large hands of revenge
Shall get my throat at last, shall get it soon,
If the joy that they are lifted to avenge
Have risen red on my night as a harvest moon,
Which even death can only put out for me;
And death, I know, is better than not-to-be.


# *Turned Down*

Hollow rang the house when I knocked at the door,
And I lingered on the threshold with my hand
Upraised to knock and knock once more;
Listening for the sound of her feet across the floor
Hollow re-echoed my heart.

The low-hung lamps stretched down the street
With people passing underneath,
With a rhythm of tapping, coming feet
To quicken my hope as I hastened to greet
The waking smile of her eyes.

The tired lights down the street went out,
The last car trailed the night behind;
And I in the darkness wandered about
With a flutter of hope and a quenching doubt
In the dying lamp of my love.

Two brown ponies trotting slowly
Stopped at a dim-lit trough to drink;
The dark van drummed down the distance lowly;
And city stars, so dim and holy,
Came nearer, to search through the streets.

A hastening car swept shameful past,
I saw her hid in the shadow;
I saw her step to the kerb, and fast
Run to the silent door, where last

I had stood with my hand uplifted.
She clung to the door in her haste to enter,
Entered, and quickly cast
It shut behind her, leaving the street aghast.

## Sickness

Waving slowly before me, pushed into the dark,
Unseen my hands explore the silence, drawing the bark
Of my body slowly behind.

Nothing to meet my fingers but the fleece of night
Invisible blinding my face and my eyes! What if in their flight
My hands should touch the door!

What if I suddenly stumble, and push the door
Open, and a great grey dawn swirls over my feet, before
I can draw back!

What if unwitting I set the door of eternity wide
And am swept away in the horrible dawn, am gone down the tide
Of eternal hereafter!

Catch my hands, my darling, between your breasts.
Take them away from their venture, before fate wrests
The meaning out of them.

## Pear-Blossom

The pear-blossom is a fountain of foam
At your cottage-end; it falls back again
In sprays and spurts of foam.

The flowers against your window pane
Are a 'poppy-show'. Peep, while you comb
Your hair, peep out on the lane!—

That year, when the pear was out, my delight
As you crawled nakèd over me,
Your small breasts clumps of white

Pear-blossom hanging! And one small knee
Dug firm in my breast as you reached out right
To the window and the white pear-tree!

And you climbed back nakèd over me
As I lay on the bed, and you sat with
                    the flowers on your thighs,
And looked at me;

As I lay and looked in your eyes
You wept, and the bed trembled under me.
I was faint with surprise—

I am terrified of the pear-blossom
Round and white as a small bosom
With a nipple centre of red:

My God, to think it is gone for ever,
To think that you are gone for ever,
I am terrified you are dead.

## Forecast

Patience, little Heart!
One day a heavy-breasted, June-hot woman
Will enter and shut the door, to stay.

And when your stifling soul would summon
Cool, lonely night, her breasts will keep the night at bay,
Leaning in your room like two tiger-lilies, curving
Their pale-gold petals back with steady will,
Killing the blue dusk with harsh scent, unnerving
Your body with their nipple-thrust, until
You thirst for coolness with a husky thirst.

And then you will remember, for the first
Time with true longing, what I was to you.
Like a wild daffodil down-dreaming,
And waiting through the blue
Chill dusk for you, and gladly gleaming
Like a little light at your feet.

Patience, little Heart! I shall be sweet
In after years, in memory, to you.

# NARRATIVES

The poems in this section were first written between 1909 and 1913. Three show Lawrence's mastery of dialect. Grief, cruelty in love and, in the two central poems, the necessity of sexual fulfilment are the themes.

# *Violets*

Sister, tha knows while we was on th' planks
    Aside o' t' grave, an' th' coffin set
On th' yaller clay, wi' th' white flowers top of it
    Waitin' ter be buried out o' th' wet?

An' t' parson makin' haste an' a' t'black
    Huddlin' up i' t' rain,
Did t' 'appen ter notice a bit of a lass way back
    Hoverin', lookin' poor an' plain?

    —How should I be lookin' round!
        An' me standin' there on th' plank,
      An' our Ted's coffin set on th' ground,
        Waitin' to be sank!

    I'd as much as I could do, to think
        Of 'im bein' gone
    That young, an' a' the fault of drink
        An' carryin's on!—

Let that be; 'appen it worna th' drink, neither,
Nor th' carryin' on as killed 'im.
                     —No, 'appen not,
My sirs! But I say 'twas! For a blither
Lad never stepped, till 'e got in with your lot.—

All right, all right, it's my fault! But let
Me tell about that lass. When you'd all gone
Ah stopped behind on t' pad, i' t' pourin' wet
An' watched what 'er 'ad on.

Tha should ha' seed 'er slive up when yer'd gone!
Tha should ha' seed 'er kneel an' look in
At th' sloppy grave! an' 'er little neck shone
That white, an' 'er cried that much, I'd like to begin

Scraightin' mysen as well. 'Er undid 'er black
Jacket at th' bosom, an' took out
Over a double 'andful o' violets, a' in a pack
An' white an' blue in a ravel, like a clout.

An' warm, for th' smell come waftin' to me. 'Er put 'er face
Right in 'em, an' scraighted a bit again,
Then after a bit 'er dropped 'em down that place,
An' I come away, acause o' th' teemin' rain.

But I thowt ter mysen, as that wor th' only bit
O' warmth as 'e got down theer; th' rest wor stone cold.
From that bit of a wench's bosom; 'e'd be glad of it,
Gladder nor of thy lilies, if tha maun be told.


# *Whether or Not*

### I

Dunna thee tell me it's his'n, mother,
   Dunna thee, dunna thee!
—Oh ay, he'll come an' tell thee his-sèn,
   Wench, wunna he?

Tha doesna mean ter say ter me, mother,
   He's gone wi' that—
—My gel, owt'll do for a man i' th' dark;
   Tha's got it flat!

But 'er's old, mother, 'er's twenty year
   Older nor him—
—Ay, an' yaller as a crowflower; an' yet i' th' dark
   Er'd do for Tim.

Tha niver believes it, does ter, mother?
   It's somebody's lies.
—Ax 'im thy-sèn, wench; a widder's lodger!
   It's no surprise.

II

A widow o' forty-five
Wi' a bitter, dirty skin,
To ha' 'ticed a lad o' twenty-five,
An' 'im to 'ave been took in!

A widow of forty-five
As 'as sludged like a horse all 'er life
Till 'er's tough as whit-leather, to slive
Atween a lad an' 'is wife!

A widow of forty-five!
A glum old otchel, wi' long
Witch teeth, an' 'er black hawk-eyes, as I've
Mistrusted all along!

An' me as 'as kep' my-sèn
Shut like a daisy bud,
Clean an' new an' nice, so's when
He wed he'd ha'e summat good!

An' 'im as nice an' fresh
As any man i' th' force,
To ha' gone an' given his clean young flesh
To a woman that coarse!

III

You're stout to brave this snow, Miss Stainwright,
        Are you makin' Brinsley way?
—I'm off up th' line to Underwood
        Wi' a dress as is wanted to-day.

Oh, are you goin' to Underwood?
        'Appen that you've 'eered!
—What's that as 'appen I've 'eered on, Missis?
        Speak up, you nedn't be feared.

Why, your young man an' Widow Naylor,
   'Er as 'e lodges wi'!
They say he's got 'er wi' childt; but there
   It's nothing to do wi' me!

Though if it's true, they'll turn 'im out
   O' th' p'lice force, without fail;
An' if it's *not* true, you may back your life
   They'll listen to *her* tale.

—Well, I'm believin' no tale, Missis,
   I'm seein' for my-sèn.
An' when I know for sure, Missis,
   I'll talk *then*.


IV

Nay, robin red-breast, tha nedna
   Sit noddin' thy head at me!
My breast's as red as thine, I reckon,
   Flayed red, if tha could but see.

Nay, yo' blessed pee-whips,
   Yo' nedna scraight at me!
I'm scraightin' my-sèn, but arena goin'
   Ter let iv'rybody see.

Tha *art* smock-ravelled, bunny,
   Larropin' neck an' crop
I' th' snow! but I's warrant thee
   *I'm* further ower th' top.


V

Now sithee theer at th' reelroad crossin'
Warmin' 'is-sèn at the stool o' fire
Under th' tank as fills th' ingines,
If there isn't my dearly-beloved liar!

My constable, wi' 'is buttoned breast
As stout as the truth, my Sirs! an' 'is face
As bold as a robin! It's much he cares
For this nice old shame an' disgrace.

Oh, but 'e drops 'is flag when 'e sees me!
Yi, an' 'is face goes white! Oh yes,
Tha can stare at me wi' thy fierce blue eyes;
Tha won't stare me out, I guess.

VI

Whativer brings thee out so far
    In a' this depth o' snow?
—I'm takin' 'ome a weddin'-dress,
    If yer mun know.

Why, is there a weddin' at Underwood
    As tha ne'd trudge up 'ere?
—It's Widder Naylor's weddin'-dress,
    'Er'll be wantin' it, I 'ear.

*'Er* doesna want no weddin'-dress—
    Why—? but what dost mean?
—Doesn't ter know what I mean, Timmy?
    Yi, tha must ha' bin 'ard ter wean!

Tha'rt a good-un at suckin'-in yet, Timmy!
    But tell me, isn't it true
As 'er'll be wantin' my weddin'-dress
    In a wik or two?

—Tha's no 'casions ter ha'e me on,
    Lizzie; what's done is done.
—*Done*, I should think so! An' might I ask
    When tha begun?

It's thee as 'as done it, as much as me,
    So there, an' I tell thee flat.
—Me gotten a childt ter thy landlady?
    —Tha's gotten thy answer pat.

As tha allus 'ast; but let me tell thee
   Hasna ter sent me whoam, when I
Was a'most burstin' mad o' myi-sèn,
   An' walkin' in agony?

After I'd kissed thee at night, Lizzie,
   An' tha's laid against me, an' melted
Into me, melted right into me, Lizzie,
   Till I was verily swelted.

An' if my landlady seed me like it.
   An' if 'er clawkin' eyes
Went through me as the light went out,
   Is it any cause for surprise?

—No cause for surprise at all, my lad;
   After kissin' an' cuddlin' wi' me, tha could
Turn thy mouth on a woman like that!
   I hope it did thee good.

—Ay, it did; but afterwards
   I could ha' killed 'er.
—Afterwards! how many times afterwards
   Could ter ha' killed 'er?

Say no more, Liz, dunna thee;
   'Er's as good as thee.
—Then I'll say good-bye to thee, Timothy;
   Take 'er i'stead o' me.

I'll ta'e thy word good-bye, Liz,
   Though I shonna marry 'er.
Nor 'er nor nub'dy.—It is
   Very brave of you, Sir!

—T' child maun ta'e its luck, it mun,
   An' 'er maun ta'e *'er* luck.
F'r I tell yer I h'arena marryin' none
   On yer; yo'n got what yer took!

—That's spoken like a man, Timmy,
  That's spoken like a man!
"E up an' fired 'is pistol,
  An' then away 'e ran!'

—I damn well shanna marry 'er,
  Nor yo', so chew it no more!
I'll chuck the flamin' lot o' you—
  —Yer nedn't 'ave swore!

### VII

There's 'is collar round th' candlestick,
An' there's the dark-blue tie I bought 'im!
An' these is the woman's kids 'e's so fond on,
An' 'ere comes the cat as caught 'im!

I dunno wheer 'is eyes was—a gret
Round-shouldered hag! My Sirs, to think
Of 'im stoopin' to 'er! You'd wonder 'e could
Throw 'imself down *that* sink!

I expect yer know who I am, Mrs. Naylor?
  —Who y'are? yis, you're Lizzie Stainwright.
An' 'appen you'd guess then what I've come for?
  —'Appen I mightn't, 'appen I might.

Yer knowed as I was courtin' Tim Merfin?
  —Yis, I knowed 'e wor courtin' thee.
An' yet yer've bin carryin' on wi' 'im!
  —Ay, an' 'im wi' me.

Well, now yer've got ter pay for it.
  —If I han, what's that ter thee?
'E isn't goin' ter marry yer.
  —Tha wants 'im thy-sèn, I see.

It 'asn't nothin' to do with me.
  —Then what art colleyfoglin' for?
*I'm* not 'avin' your orts an' slarts.
  —Which on us said yon wor?

But I want you to know 'e's not *marryin'* you.
   —Tha wants 'im thy-sèn too bad.
Though I'll see as 'e pays you, an' does what's rig
   —Tha'rt for doin' a lot wi' t' lad!


VIII

To think I should 'ave ter 'affle an' caffle
   Wi' a woman, an' name 'er a price
For lettin' me marry the lad as I thought
   Ter marry wi' cabs an' rice!

But we'll go unbeknown ter th' registrar,
   An' give *'er* the money there is;
For I won't be beholden to such as 'er,
   I won't, or my name's not Liz.


IX

Ta'e off thy duty stripes, Tim,
   An' come in 'ere wi' me;
Ta'e off thy p'liceman's helmet
   An' look at me.

I wish tha hadna done it, Tim,
   I do an' that I do!
For whenever I look thee i' th' face, I s'll see
   Her face too.

I wish I could wesh 'er off'n thee;
   'Appen I can, if I try.
But tha'll ha'e ter promise ter be true ter me
   Till I die. . . .


X

Twenty pound o' thy own tha hast, an' fifty pound ha'e I;
Thine shall go ter pay the woman, an' wi' my bit we'll buy
All as we s'll want for furniture when tha leaves this place;
An' we'll be married at th'registrar—now lift thy face!

Lift thy face an' look at me, man! canna ter look at me?
Sorry I am for this business, an' sorry if ever I've driven thee
To do such a thing; though it's a poor tale, it is, that I'm bound to
    say,
Afore I can ta'e thee I've got a widder o' forty-five ter pay!

Dunnat thee think but what I've loved thee; I've loved thee too well.
An' 'deed an' I wish as this tale o' thine wor niver my tale to tell!
Deed an' I wish I c'd 'a' stood at th' altar wi' thee an' bin proud o'
    thee!
That I could 'a' bin first woman ter thee, as tha'rt first man ter me!

But we maun ma'e the best on't. So now rouse up an' look at me.
Look up an' say tha'rt sorry tha did it; say tha'rt sorry for me.
They'll turn thee out o' th' force, I doubt me; if they do, we can see
If my father can get thee a job on t'bank. Say tha'rt sorry, Timmy!

                          XI
        Ay, I'm sorry, I'm sorry,
            But what o' that!
        Ay, I'm sorry! Tha nedna worry
            Nor fret thy fat.

        I'm sorry for thee, I'm sorry f'r 'er,
            I'm sorry f'r us a'.
        But what then? Tha wants me, does ter
            After a'?

        Ah'n put my-sèn i' th' wrong, Liz,
            An' 'er as well.
        An' tha'rt that right, tha knows; 'tis
            Other folks in hell.

        Tha *art* so sure tha'rt right, Liz!
            That damned sure!
        But 'ark thee 'ere, that widder woman
            's less graspin', if 'er's poor.

What 'er gen, 'er gen me
   Beout a thought.
'Er gen me summat; I shanna
   Say it wor nought.

I'm sorry for th' trouble, ay
   As comes on us a'.
But sorry for what I had? why
   I'm not that's a.

As for marryin', I shanna marry
   Neither on yer.
Ah've 'ad a' as I can carry
   From you an' from 'er.

So I s'll go an' leave yer,
   Both on yer.
I don't like yer, Liz, I want ter
   Get away from yer.

An' I really like 'er neither,
   Even though I've 'ad
More from 'er than from you; but either
   Of yer's too much for this lad.

Let me go! what's good o'talkin'?
   Let's a' ha' done.
Talk about love o' women!
   Ter me it's no fun.

What bit o' cunt I had wi'er
   's all I got out of it.
An' 's not good enough, it isn't
   For a permanent fit.

I'll say good-bye, Liz, to yer,
   Yer too much i' th' right for me.
An' wi' er somehow it isn't right.
   So good-bye, an' let's let be!

# The Drained Cup

T' snow is witherin' off'n th' gress—
  Lad, should I tell thee summat?
T' snow is witherin' off'n th' gress
An' mist is suckin' at th' spots o' snow,
An' ower a' the thaw an' mess
There's a moon, full blow.
  Lad, but I'm tellin' thee summat!

Tha's bin snowed up i' this cottage wi' me—
  'Ark, tha'rt for hearin' summat!
Tha's bin snowed up i' this cottage wi' me
While t' clocks 'as a' run down an' stopped,
An' t' short days goin' unknown ter thee
Unbeknown has dropped.
  Yi, but I'm tellin' thee summat.

How many days dost think has gone?
  Now, lad, I'm axin' thee summat.
How many days dost think has gone?
How many times has t' candle-light shone
On thy face as tha got more white an' wan?
  —Seven days, my lad, or none!
    Aren't ter hearin' summat?

Tha come ter say good-bye ter me,
  Tha wert frit o' summat.
Tha come ter ha' finished an' done wi' me
An' off to a gel as wor younger than me,
An' fresh an' more nicer for marryin' wi—
  Yi, but tha'rt frit o'summat.

Ah wunna kiss thee, tha trembles so!
    Tha'rt daunted, or summat.
Tha arena very flig ter go.
Dost want me ter want thee again? Nay though,
There's hardly owt left o' thee; get up an' go!
    Or dear o' me, say summat.

Tha wanted ter leave me that bad, tha knows!
    Doesn't ter know it?
But tha wanted me more ter want thee, so's
Tha could let thy very soul out. A man
Like thee can't rest till his last spunk goes
Out of 'im into a woman as can
    Draw it out of 'im. Did ter know it?

Tha thought tha wanted a little wench,
    Ay, lad I'll tell thee thy mind.
Tha thought tha wanted a little wench
As 'ud make thee a wife an' look up ter thee.
As 'ud wince when tha touched 'er close, an'
    blench
An' lie frightened ter death under thee.
    She worn't hard ter find.

Tha thought tha wanted ter be rid 'o me.
    'Appen tha did, an' a'.
Tha thought tha wanted ter marry an' see
If ter couldna be master an' th' woman's boss.
Tha'd need a woman different from me,
An' tha knowed it; ay, yet tha comes across
    Ter say good-bye! an' a'.

I tell thee tha won't be satisfied,
    Tha might as well listen, tha knows.
I tell thee tha won't be satisfied
Till a woman has drawn the last last drop
O' thy spunk, an' tha'rt empty an' mortified.
Empty an' empty from bottom to top.
    It's true, tha knows.

Tha'rt one o' th' men as has got to drain
   —An' I've loved thee for it,
Their blood in a woman, to the very last vein.
Tha *must*, though tha tries ter get away.
Tha wants it, and everything else is in vain.
   An' a woman like me loves thee for it.

Maun tha cling to the wa' as tha stan's?
   Ay, an' tha maun.
An' tha looks at me, an' tha understan's.
Yi, tha can go. Tha hates me now.
But tha'lt come again. Because when a man's
Not finished, he hasn't, no matter how.
   Go then, sin' tha maun.

Tha come ter say good-bye ter me.
   Now go then, now then go.
It's ta'en thee seven days ter day it ter me.
Now go an' marry that wench, an' see
How long it'll be afore tha'lt be
Weary an' sick o' the likes o' she,
   An' hankerin' for me. But go!

A woman's man tha art, ma lad,
   But it's my sort o' woman.
Go then, tha'lt ha'e no peace till ter's had
A go at t'other, for I'm a bad
Sort o' woman for any lad.
   —Ay, it's a rum un!

# The Young Soldier with Bloody Spurs

### A Servant Girl Speaks

The sergeant says that eight and twenty wagons
Are coming behind, and we must put out all
The water we can at the gate, for the horses.—He gallops
To the next farm, pulls up where the elder flowers fall.

The wheat on both sides of the road stands green,
And hundreds of soldiers on horseback have filed between
It, gone by our farm to the mountains that stand back blue
This morning.

       I think perhaps the man that came
To Wolfratshausen last winter's end, comes through
This place today. These soldiers wear the same
Helmets as his he lost in the wood that night,
And their uniforms are the same of white and blue——

It was cold, and he put his cloak right round me
As we walked; dark, so he held his arm close round me.
In the stillness, he took off his helmet to kiss me——
It snowed, and his helmet was lost, he forgot me, he did not
    miss me.

The Isar whispers again in the valley; the children
Are ducking their heads in the water tubs at the gate
As they go from school; some of the officers rally
At the door of the Gasthaus down the road: great
Threads of blue wind far, and down the road
I wait for the eight and twenty wagons to come.

At last I hear a rattle, and there away
Crawls the first load into sight—and now there are some
Drawing near, they cover the München road,
                     Nay,
I dread him coming; I wonder how he will take it.
I can see his raging black eyes blaze at me
And feel him gripping my wrist as if he would break it.

Here comes the first of the wagons, a grey, a dreary
Shut-up coffin of a thing, with a soldier weary
In the box, and four hot horses going drearily,
And a soldier in the saddle of the left-hand draught-horse, sitting
    wearily.

One by one they go by—at last
There he sits in the saddle of this the five
And twentieth wagon.—And he will not drive past
He pulls up for our water; would he drive
On if he knew that *I* was at this farm?

And he swings his heavy thigh
Out of the saddle, and staggering
With stiffness comes for the water that I
Have poured for the horses—a dark-blue, staggering
Strong young man.—He leans sighing
With head against the shaft, and takes
His helmet off, and wipes his hair, trying
To ease himself in his clothes. It makes
Me want to cry, to see him so strong and easy,
Swarthy and strong with his damp thick hair
Pushed up on end—and the breath sighing
Between his thick lips.—I wonder where
He thinks I am—if ever he thinks at all.
But his handkerchief is white with a broad blue border,
A nice one, I like it.—He'll think it's a tall order
When I say he ought to marry me.—And small
I feel to have to tell him.

                              But why, before
He waters the horses, does he wash his heel?
Jesus!—his spurs are red with shining blood!

He splashes water from the pail upon them,
And rubs the silver clean with his thick brown fingers,
Bending backwards awkwardly,
And anxiously, like a boy afraid to be found out.

And he goes and washes the belly of the horse,
A poor roan thing: its hind leg twitches
Forwards as he rubs the wound,
And bloody water falls upon the road
Soiling the clean white dust.—He rubs the belly
Carefully again, and again, to stop the bleeding.
Jesus!—his fingers are red!

And again, rolling in his heavy high boots,
He comes to the side of the road and washes his hand,
And looks round again at his heel, the bright spur,
And bends again and looks at the belly of the horse,
And kicks dust over the red stain in the road.

And all the time his handsome, swarthy red face
With savage black eyes is sulky: and all the time
He frowns as if he were worried, as if the place
On the horse's belly hurt him, for he was rather gentle
To the thing, and rather fretted. And his thick black hair
Was wet with sweat, and his movements strong and heavy.
—I wonder, will he care!

Now I take the big stone jug of water
Down to the gate, and stand and wait
For a word. He is coming towards the gate—
His eyes meet mine as he takes the jug of water,
He knows me, but does not speak: instead
He drinks and drinks, then turns away his head.

'Do you remember me?'
—'Yes!'
'Who then?'
—'Maria, of the Gasthaus Green Hat, Wolfratshausen.'
'I am with child by you——'

He looked at me, and his heavy brows came over
His eyes and he sulked.—He had another lover.

'It is true,' I said.
—'And what do you want?'
'What do you think?' I said.

He looked away down the road.

Suddenly his horses began to start.
He shouted, ran heavily after them,
And jerked back their bridles, pushing their heads apart.

I waited, but he would not come back to me,
He stayed with the horses, sulkily,
Till the whistle went.—Then swiftly he

Swung strong and heavy to saddle again
And called to his horses, and his strong blue body
Had its back to me;
And away went the last of the wagons.

# THE VIRGIN MOTHER

The poems in this section are Lawrence's elegaic love poems about his mother, and their first composition dates, in the main, from the time of her illness (August 1910 onwards) or the days immediately after her death from cancer on 9 December 1910. She was aged fifty-nine.

# Discord in Childhood

Outside the house an ash-tree hung its terrible whips,
And at night when the wind rose, the lash of the tree
Shrieked and slashed the wind, as a ship's
Weird rigging in a storm shrieks hideously.

Within the house two voices arose, a slender lash
Whistling she-delirious rage, and the dreadful sound
Of a male thong booming and bruising, until it had
    drowned
The other voice in a silence of blood, 'neath the noise
    of the ash.

# Monologue of a Mother

This is the last of all, then, this is the last!
I must fold my hands, and turn my face to the fire,
And watch my dead days fusing together in dross,
Shape after shape, and scene after scene of my past
Clotting to one dead mass in the sinking fire
Where ash on the dying coals grows swiftly, like heavy moss.

Strange he is, my son, for whom I have waited like a lover;
Strange to me, like a captive in a foreign country, haunting
The confines, gazing out beyond, where the winds go free;
White and gaunt, with wistful eyes that hover
Always on the distance, as if his soul were chaunting
A monotonous weird of departure away from me.

Like a thin white bird blown out of the northern seas,
Like a bird from the far north blown with a broken wing
Into our sooty garden, he drags and beats
Along the fence perpetually, seeking release
From me, from the hand of my love which creeps up, needing
His happiness, whilst he in displeasure retreats.

I must look away from him, for my faded eyes
Like a cringing dog at his heels offend him now,
Like a toothless hound pursuing him with my will;
Till he chafes at my crouching persistence, and a sharp spark flies
In my soul from under the sudden frown of his brow
As he blenches and turns away, and my heart stands still.

This is the last, it will not be any more.
All my life I have borne the burden of myself,
All the long years of sitting in my husband's house;
Never have I said to myself as he closed the door:
'Now I am caught! You are hopelessly lost, O Self!
You are frightened with joy, my heart, like a frightened mouse.'

Three times have I offered myself, three times rejected.
It will not be any more. No more, my son, my son!—
Never to know the glad freedom of obedience, since long ago
The angel of childhood kissed me and went! I expected
This last one to claim me;—and now, my son, O my son,
I must sit alone and wait, and never know
The loss of myself, till death comes, who cannot fail.

Death, in whose service is nothing of gladness, takes me;
For the lips and the eyes of God are behind a veil.
And the thought of the lipless voice of the Father shakes me
With dread, and fills my heart with the tears of desire,
And my heart rebels with anguish, as night draws nigher.

# *End of Another Home Holiday*

When shall I see the half-moon sink again
Behind the black sycamore at the end of the garden?
When will the scent of the dim white phlox
Creep up the wall to me, and in at my open window?

Why is it, the long, slow stroke of the midnight bell
   (Will it never finish the twelve?)
Falls again and again on my heart with a heavy reproach?

The moon-mist is over the village, out of the mist speaks the bell,
And all the little roofs of the village bow low, pitiful, beseeching,
   resigned.
—Speak, you my home! what is it I don't do well?

Ah home, suddenly I love you
As I hear the sharp clean trot of a pony down the road,
Succeeding sharp little sounds dropping into silence
Clear upon the long-drawn hoarseness of a train across the valley.

*

The light has gone out, from under my mother's door.
   That she should love me so!—
   She, so lonely, greying now!
   And I leaving her,
   Bent on my pursuits!

      Love is the great Asker.
      The sun and the rain do not ask the secret
      Of the time when the grain struggles down in the dark.
      The moon walks her lonely way without anguish,
      Because no-one grieves over her departure.

Forever, ever by my shoulder pitiful love will linger,
Crouching as little houses crouch under the mist when I turn.
Forever, out of the mist, the church lifts up a reproachful finger,
Pointing my eyes in wretched defiance where love hides her face to
   mourn.

      Oh! but the rain creeps down to wet the grain
      That struggles alone in the dark,
      And asking nothing, patiently steals back again!
      The moon sets forth o' nights
      To walk the lonely, dusky heights

Serenely, with steps unswerving;
Pursued by no sigh of bereavement.
No tears of love unnerving
Her constant tread:
While ever at my side,
Frail and sad, with grey, bowed head,
The beggar-woman, the yearning-eyed
Inexorable love goes lagging.

The wild young heifer, glancing distraught,
With a strange new knocking of life at her side
    Runs seeking a loneliness.
The little grain draws down the earth, to hide.
Nay, even the slumberous egg, as it labours under the shell
    Patiently to divide and self-divide,
Asks to be hidden, and wishes nothing to tell.

But when I draw the scanty cloak of silence over my eyes
Piteous love comes peering under the hood;
Touches the clasp with trembling fingers, and tries
To put her ear to the painful sob of my blood;
While her tears soak through to my breast.
    Where they burn and cauterise.

\*

The moon lies back and reddens.
In the valley a corncrake calls
    Monotonously,
With a plaintive, unalterable voice, that deadens
    My confident activity;
With a hoarse, insistent request that falls
    Unweariedly, unweariedly,
    Asking something more of me,
        Yet more of me.

# The Bride

My love looks like a girl to-night,
　　But she is old.
The plaits that lie along her pillow
　　Are not gold,
But threaded with filigree silver,
　　And uncanny cold.

She looks like a young maiden, since her brow
　　Is smooth and fair;
Her cheeks are very smooth, her eyes are closed,
　　She sleeps a rare,
Still, winsome sleep, so still, and so composed.

Nay, but she sleeps like a bride, and dreams her dreams
　　Of perfect things.
She lies at last, the darling, in the shape of her dream;
　　And her dead mouth sings
By its shape, like thrushes in clear evenings.

# The Virgin Mother

My little love, my darling,
You were a doorway to me;
You let me out of the confines
Into this strange countrie
Where people are crowded like thistles,
Yet are shapely and comely to see.

My little love, my dearest,
Twice you have issued me,
Once from your womb, sweet mother,
Once from your soul, to be
Free of all hearts, my darling,
Of each heart's entrance free.

And so, my love, my mother,
I shall always be true to you.
Twice I am born, my dearest:
To life, and to death, in you;
And this is the life hereafter
Wherein I am true.

I kiss you good-bye, my darling,
Our ways are different now;
You are a seed in the night-time,
I am a man, to plough
The difficult glebe of the future
For seed to endow.

I kiss you good-bye, my dearest,
It is finished between us here.
Oh, if I were calm as you are,
Sweet and still on your bier!
Oh God, if I had not to leave you
Alone, my dear!

Is the last word now uttered?
Is the farewell said?
Spare me the strength to leave you
Now you are dead.
I must go, but my soul lies helpless
Beside your bed.

## Sorrow

Why does the thin grey strand
Floating up from the forgotten
Cigarette between my fingers,
Why does it trouble me?

Ah, you will understand;
When I carried my mother downstairs,
A few times only, at the beginning
Of her soft-foot malady,

I should find, for a reprimand
To my gaiety, a few long grey hairs
On the breast of my coat; and one by one
I watched them float up the dark chimney.

# *Listening*

I listen to the stillness of you,
   My dear, among it all;
I feel your silence touch my words as I talk
   And hold them in thrall.

My words fly off a forge
   The length of a spark;
I see the silence easily sip them
   Up in the dark.

The lark sings loud and glad,
   Yet I am not loth
That silence should take the song and the bird
   And lose them both.

A train goes roaring south,
   The steam-flag flowing;
I see the stealthy shadow of silence
   Alongside going.

And off the forge of the world
   Whirling in the draught of life
Go myriad sparks of people, filling
   The night with strife.

Yet they never change the darkness
   Nor blench it with noise;
Alone on the perfect silence
   The stars are buoys.


# *Piano*

Softly, in the dusk, a woman is singing to me;
Taking me back down the vista of years, till I see
A child sitting under the piano, in the boom of the tingling strings
And pressing the small, poised feet of a mother who smiles as
   she sings.

In spite of myself, the insidious mastery of song
Betrays me back, till the heart of me weeps to belong
To the old Sunday evenings at home, with winter outside
And hymns in the cosy parlour, the tinkling piano our guide.

So now it is vain for the singer to burst into clamour
With the great black piano appassionato. The glamour
Of childish days is upon me, my manhood is cast
Down in the flood of remembrance, I weep like a child for the past.

# FROM
## *LOOK! WE HAVE COME THROUGH!*

These poems were first written in 1912–14, and deal with Lawrence's fiercely committed but difficult relationship with Frieda Weekley, leading up to their marriage. Memories of his mother, and moments of self-dedication to her memory, also appear.

# Hymn to Priapus

My love lies underground
With her face upturned to mine,
And her mouth unclosed in a last long kiss
That ended her life and mine.

I dance at the Christmas party
Under the mistletoe
Along with a ripe, slack country lass
Jostling to and fro.

The big, soft country lass,
Like a loose sheaf of wheat
Slipped through my arms on the threshing floor
At my feet.

The warm, soft country lass,
Sweet as an armful of wheat
At threshing-time broken, was broken
For me, and ah, it was sweet!

Now I am going home
Fulfilled and alone,
I see the great Orion standing
Looking down.

He's the star of my first beloved
Love-making.
The witness of all that bitter-sweet
Heart-aching.

Now he sees this as well,
This last commission.
Nor do I get any look
Of admonition.

He can add the reckoning up
I suppose, between now and then,
Having walked himself in the thorny, difficult
Ways of men.

He has done as I have done
No doubt:
Remembered and forgotten
Turn and about.

My love lies underground
With her face upturned to mine,
And her mouth unclosed in the last long kiss
That ended her life and mine.

She fares in the stark immortal
Fields of death;
I in these goodly, frozen
Fields beneath.

Something in me remembers
And will not forget.
The stream of my life in the darkness
Deathward set!

And someting in me has forgotten,
Has ceased to care.
Desire comes up, and contentment
Is debonair.

I, who am worn and careful,
How much do I care?
How is it I grin then, and chuckle
Over despair?

Grief, grief, I suppose and sufficient
Grief makes us free
To be faithless and faithful together
As we have to be.

# Ballad of a Wilful Woman

### First Part

Upon her plodding palfrey
With a heavy child at her breast
And Joseph holding the bridle
They mount to the last hill-crest.

Dissatisfied and weary
She sees the blade of the sea
Dividing earth and heaven
In a glitter of ecstasy.

Sudden a dark-faced stranger,
With his back to the sun, holds out
His arms; so she lights from her palfrey
And turns her round about.

She has given the child to Joseph,
Gone down to the flashing shore;
And Joseph, shading his eyes with his hand,
Stands watching evermore.

### Second Part

The sea in the stones is singing,
A woman binds her hair
With yellow, frail sea-poppies,
That shine as her fingers stir.

While a naked man comes swiftly
Like a spurt of white foam rent
From the crest of a falling breaker,
Over the poppies sent.

He puts his surf-wet fingers
Over her startled eyes,
And asks if she sees the land, the land,
The land of her glad surmise.


## *Third Part*

Again in her blue, blue mantle
Riding at Joseph's side,
She says, 'I went to Cythera,
And woe betide!'

Her heart is a swinging cradle
That holds the perfect child,
But the shade on her forehead ill becomes
A mother mild.

So on with the slow, mean journey
In the pride of humility;
Till they halt at a cliff on the edge of the land
Over a sullen sea.

While Joseph pitches the sleep-tent
She goes far down to the shore
To where a man in a heaving boat
Waits with a lifted oar.


## *Fourth Part*

They dwelt in a huge, hoarse sea-cave
And looked far down the dark
Where an archway torn and glittering
Shone like a huge sea-spark.

He said: 'Do you see the spirits
Crowding the bright doorway?'
He said: 'Do you hear them whispering?'
He said: 'Do you catch what they say?'

## Fifth Part

Then Joseph, grey with waiting,
His dark eyes full of pain,
Heard: 'I have been to Patmos;
Give me the child again.'

Now on with the hopeless journey
Looking bleak ahead she rode,
And the man and the child of no more account
Than the earth the palfrey trode.

Till a beggar spoke to Joseph,
But looked into her eyes;
So she turned, and said to her husband:
'I give, whoever denies.'

## Sixth Part

She gave on the open heather
Beneath bare judgment stars,
And she dreamed of her children and Joseph,
And the isles, and her men, and her scars.

And she woke to distil the berries
The beggar had gathered at night,
Whence he drew the curious liquors
He held in delight.

He gave her no crown of flowers,
No child and no palfrey slow,
Only led her through harsh, hard places
Where strange winds blow.

She follows his restless wanderings
Till night when, by the fire's red stain,
Her face is bent in the bitter steam
That comes from the flowers of pain.

Then merciless and ruthless
He takes the flame-wild drops
To the town and tries to sell them
With the market-crops.

So she follows the cruel journey
That ends not anywhere,
And dreams, as she stirs the mixing-pot,
She is brewing hope from despair.

*Trier.*

# Bei Hennef

The little river twittering in the twilight,
The wan, wondering look of the pale sky,
  This is almost bliss.

And everything shut up and gone to sleep,
All the troubles and anxieties and pain
  Gone under the twilight.

Only the twilight now, and the soft 'Sh!' of the river
  That will last for ever.

And at last I know my love for you is here;
I can see it all, it is whole like the twilight,
It is large, so large, I could not see it before,
Because of the little lights and flickers and interruptions,
  Troubles, anxieties and pains.

You are the call and I am the answer,
You are the wish, and I the fulfilment,
You are the night, and I the day.
   What else? it is perfect enough.
   It is perfectly complete,
   You and I,
   What more——?

Strange, how we suffer in spite of this!

*Hennef am Rhein.*


# First Morning

The night was a failure
   but why not——?

In the darkness
   with the pale dawn seething at the window
   through the black frame
   I could not be free,
   not free myself from the past, those others—
   and our love was a confusion,
   there was a horror,
   you recoiled away from me.

Now, in the morning
As we sit in the sunshine on the seat by the little shrine,
And look at the mountain-walls,
Walls of blue shadow,
And see so near at our feet in the meadow
Myriads of dandelion pappus
Bubbles ravelled in the dark green grass
Held still beneath the sunshine—
It is enough, you are near—
The mountains are balanced,
The dandelion seeds stay half-submerged in the grass;
You and I together

We hold them proud and blithe
On our love.
They stand upright on our love,
Everything starts from us,
We are the source.

*Beuerberg.*

## *Frohnleichnam*

You have come your way, I have come my way;
You have stepped across your people, carelessly, hurting them all;
I have stepped across my people, and hurt them in spite of my care.
But steadily, surely, and notwithstanding
We have come our ways and met at last
Here in this upper room.

Here the balcony
Overhangs the street where the bullock-wagons slowly
Go by with their loads of green and silver birch-trees
For the feast of Corpus Christi.

Here from the balcony
We look over the growing wheat, where the jade-green river
Goes between the pine-woods,
Over and beyond to where the many mountains
Stand in their blueness, flashing with snow and the morning.

I have done; a quiver of exultation goes through me, like the first
Breeze of the morning through a narrow white birch.
You glow at last like the mountain tops when they catch
Day and make magic in heaven.

At last I can throw away world without end, and meet you
Unsheathed and naked and narrow and white;
At last you can throw immortality off, and I see you
Glistening with all the moment and all your beauty.

Shameless and callous I love you;
Out of indifference I love you;
Out of mockery we dance together,
Out of the sunshine into the shadow,
Passing across the shadow into the sunlight,
Out of sunlight to shadow.

As we dance
Your eyes take all of me in as a communication:
As we dance
I see you, ah, in full!
Only to dance together in triumph of being together
Two white ones, sharp, vindicated,
Shining and touching,
Is heaven of our own, sheer with repudiation.

# A Young Wife

The pain of loving you
Is almost more than I can bear.

I walk in fear of you.
The darkness starts up where
You stand, and the night comes through
Your eyes when you look at me.

Ah never before did I see
The shadows that live in the sun!

Now every tall glad tree
Turns round its back to the sun
And looks down on the ground, to see
The shadow it used to shun.

At the foot of each glowing thing
A night lies looking up.

Oh, and I want to sing
And dance, but I can't lift up
My eyes from the shadows: dark
They lie spilt round the cup.

What is it?—Hark
The faint fine seethe in the air!

Like the seething sound in a shell!
It is death still seething where
The wild-flower shakes its bell
And the skylark twinkles blue—

The pain of loving you
Is almost more than I can bear.

# Green

The dawn was apple-green,
   The sky was green wine held up in the sun,
The moon was a golden petal between.

She opened her eyes, and green
   They shone, clear like flowers undone
For the first time, now for the first time seen.
*Icking.*

# Gloire de Dijon

When she rises in the morning
I linger to watch her;
She spreads the bath-cloth underneath the window
And the sunbeams catch her
Glistening white on the shoulders,
While down her sides the mellow

Golden shadow glows as
She stoops to the sponge, and her swung breasts
Sway like full-blown yellow
Gloire de Dijon roses.

She drips herself with water, and her shoulders
Glisten as silver, they crumple up
Like wet and falling roses, and I listen
For the sluicing of their rain-dishevelled petals.
In the window full of sunlight
Concentrates her golden shadow
Fold on fold, until it glows as
Mellow as the glory roses.

*Icking.*


## Roses on the Breakfast Table

Just a few of the roses we gathered from the Isar
Are fallen, and their mauve-red petals on the cloth
Float like boats on a river, while other
Roses are ready to fall, reluctant and loth.

She laughs at me across the table, saying
I am beautiful. I look at the rumpled young roses
And suddenly realize, in them as in me,
How lovely is the self this day discloses.


## I am Like a Rose

I am myself at last; now I achieve
My very self. I, with the wonder mellow,
Full of fine warmth, I issue forth in clear
And single me, perfected from my fellow.

Here I am all myself. No rose-bush heaving
Its limpid sap to culmination has brought
Itself more sheer and naked out of the green
In stark-clear roses, than I to myself am brought.

# Rose of all the World

I am here myself; as though this heave of effort
At starting other life, fulfilled my own:
Rose-leaves that whirl in colour round a core
Of seed-specks kindled lately and softly blown

By all the blood of the rose-bush into being—
Strange, that the urgent will in me, to set
My mouth on hers in kisses, and so softly
To bring together two strange sparks, beget

Another life from our lives, so should send
The innermost fire of my own dim soul out-spinning
And whirling in blossom of flame and being upon me!
That my completion of manhood should be the beginning

Another life from mine! For so it looks.
The seed is purpose, blossom accident.
The seed is all in all, the blossom lent
To crown the triumph of this new descent.

Is that it, woman? Does it strike you so?
The Great Breath blowing a tiny seed of fire
Fans out your petals for excess of flame,
Till all your being smokes with fine desire?

Or are we kindled, you and I, to be
One rose of wonderment upon the tree
Of perfect life, and is our possible seed
But the residuum of the ecstasy?

How will you have it?—the rose is all in all,
Or the ripe rose-fruits of the luscious fall?
The sharp begetting, or the child begot?
Our consummation matters, or does it not?

To me it seems the seed is just left over
From the red rose-flowers' fiery transience;
Just orts and slarts; berries that smoulder in the bush
Which burnt just now with marvellous immanence.

Blossom, my darling, blossom, be a rose
Of roses unchidden and purposeless; a rose
For rosiness only, without an ulterior motive;
For me it is more than enough if the flower unclose.

## *Quite Forsaken*

What pain, to wake and miss you!
    To wake with a tightened heart,
And mouth reaching forward to kiss you!

This then at last is the dawn, and the bell
    Clanging at the farm! Such bewilderment
Comes with the sight of the room, I cannot tell.

It is raining. Down the half-obscure road
    Four labourers pass with their scythes
Dejectedly;—a huntsman goes by with his load:

A gun, and a bunched-up deer, its four little feet
    Clustered dead.—And this is the dawn
For which I wanted the night to retreat!

# A Doe at Evening

As I went through the marshes
a doe sprang out of the corn
and flashed up the hill-side
leaving her fawn.

On the sky-line
she moved round to watch,
she picked a fine black blotch
on the sky.

I looked at her
and felt her watching;
I became a strange being.
Still, I had my right to be there with her.

Her nimble shadow trotting
along the sky-line, she
put back her fine, level-balanced head.
And I knew her.

Ah yes, being male, is not my head hard-
    balanced, antlered?
Are not my haunches light?
Has she not fled on the same wind with me?
Does not my fear cover her fear?

*Irschenhausen.*

# Sinners

The big mountains sit still in the afternoon light,
    Shadows in their lap;
The bees roll round in the wild-thyme with delight.

We sitting here among the cranberries
    So still in the gap
Of rock, distilling our memories,

Are sinners! Strange! The bee that blunders
   Against me goes off with a laugh.
A squirrel cocks his head on the fence, and wonders

What about sin?—For, it seems
   The mountains have
No shadow of us on their snowy forehead of dreams

As they ought to have. They rise above us
   Dreaming
For ever. One even might think that they love us.

   *Little red cranberries cheek to cheek,*
   *Two great dragon-flies wrestling;*
   *You, with your forehead nestling*
   *Against me, and bright peak shining to peak—*

There's a love-song for you!—Ah, if only
   There were no teeming
Swarms of mankind in the world, and we were less lonely!
                  *Mayrhofen.*

# *Everlasting Flowers for a Dead Mother*

Who do you think stands watching
   The snow-tops shining rosy
In heaven, now that the darkness
   Takes all but the tallest posy?

Who then sees the two-winged
   Boat down there, all alone
And asleep on the snow's last shadow,
   Like a moth on a stone?

The olive-leaves, light as gad-flies,
   Have all gone dark, gone black.
And now in the dark my soul to you
   Turns back.

To you, my little darling,
   To you, out of Italy.
For what is loveliness, my love,
   Save you have it with me!

So, there's an oxen wagon
   Comes darkly into sight:
A man with a lantern, swinging
   A little light.

What does he see, my darling,
   Here by the darkened lake?
Here, in the sloping shadow
   The mountains make?

He says not a word, but passes,
   Staring at what he sees.
What ghost of us both do you think he saw
   Under the olive-trees?

All the things that are lovely—
   The things you never knew—
I wanted to gather them one by one
   And bring them to you.

But never now, my darling,
   Can I gather the mountain-tips
From the twilight like half-shut lilies
   To hold to your lips.

And never the two-winged vessel
   That sleeps below on the lake
Can I catch like a moth between my hands
   For you to take.

But hush, I am not regretting:
   It is far more perfect now.
I'll whisper the ghostly truth to you
   And tell you how

I know you here in the darkness,
    How you sit in the throne of my eyes
At peace, and look out of the windows
    In glad surprise.

                                    *Lago di Garda.*


## Sunday Afternoon in Italy

The man and the maid go side by side
With an interval of space between;
And his hands are awkward and want to hide,
She braves it out since she must be seen.

When some one passes he drops his head,
Shading his face in his black felt hat,
While the hard girl hardens; nothing is said,
There is nothing to wonder or cavil at.

Alone on the open road again,
With the mountain snows across the lake
Flushing the afternoon, they are uncomfortable,
The loneliness daunts them, their stiff throats ache.

And he sighs with relief when she parts from him;
Her proud head held in its black silk scarf
Gone under the archway, home, he can join
The men that lounge in a group on the wharf.

His evening is a flame of wine
Among the eager, cordial men.
And she with her women hot and hard
Moves at her ease again.

    *She is marked, she is singled out*
            *For the fire:*
    *The brand is upon him, look you!*
            *Of desire.*

*They are chosen, ah, they are fated*
  *For the fight!*
*Champion her, all you women! Men, menfolk,*
  *Hold him your light!*

*Nourish her, train her, harden her,*
  *Women all!*
*Fold him, be good to him, cherish him,*
  *Men, ere he fall.*

*Women, another champion!*
  *This, men, is yours!*
*Wreathe and enlap and anoint them*
  *Behind separate doors.*

                                    *Gargnano.*


# *All Souls*

They are chanting now the service of All the Dead
And the village folk outside in the burying-ground
Listen—except those who strive with their dead,
Reaching out in anguish, yet unable quite to touch them:
Those villagers isolated at the grave
Where the candles burn in the daylight, and the painted wreaths
Are propped on end, there, where the mystery starts.

The naked candles burn on every grave.
On your grave, in England, the weeds grow.

But I am your naked candle burning,
And that is not your grave, in England,
The world is your grave.
And my naked body standing on your grave
Upright towards heaven is burning off to you
Its flame of life, now and always, till the end.

It is my offering to you; every day is All Souls' Day.

I forget you, have forgotten you.
I am busy only at my burning,
I am busy only at my life.
But my feet are on your grave, planted.
And when I lift my face, it is a flame that goes up
To the other world, where you are now.
But I am not concerned with you.
          I have forgotten you.

I am a naked candle burning on your grave.


## Both Sides of the Medal

And because you love me,
think you you do not hate me?
Ha, since you love me
to ecstasy
it follows you hate me to ecstasy.

Because when you hear me
go down the road outside the house
you must come to the window to watch me go,
do you think it is pure worship?

Because, when I sit in the room,
here, in my own house,
and you want to enlarge yourself with this friend of mine,
such a friend as he is,
yet you cannot get beyond your awareness of me,
you are held back by my being in the same world with you,
do you think it is bliss alone?
sheer harmony?

No doubt if I were dead, you must
reach into death after me,
but would not your hate reach even more madly than your love?
your impassioned, unfinished hate?

Since you have a passion for me,
as I for you,
does not that passion stand in your way like a Balaam's ass?
and am I not Balaam's ass
golden-mouthed occasionally?
But mostly, do you not detest my bray?

Since you are confined in the orbit of me
do you not loathe the confinement?
Is not even the beauty and peace of an orbit
an intolerable prison to you,
as it is to everybody?

But we will learn to submit
each of us to the balanced, eternal orbit
wherein we circle on our fate
in strange conjunction.

What is chaos, my love?
It is not freedom.
A disarray of falling stars coming to nought.

# Loggerheads

Please yourself how you have it.
Take my words, and fling
Them down on the counter roundly;
See if they ring.

Sift my looks and expressions,
And see what proportion there is
Of sand in my doubtful sugar
Of verities.

Have a real stock-taking
Of my manly breast;
Find out if I'm sound or bankrupt,
Or a poor thing at best.

For I am quite indifferent
To your dubious state,
As to whether you've found a fortune
In me, or a flea-bitten fate.

Make a good investigation
Of all that is there,
And then, if it's worth it, be grateful—
If not, then despair.

If despair is our portion
Then let us despair.
Let us make for the weeping willow.
I don't care.


# *December Night*

Take off your cloak and your hat
And your shoes, and draw up at my hearth
Where never woman sat.

I have made the fire up bright;
Let us leave the rest in the dark
And sit by firelight.

The wine is warm in the hearth;
The flickers come and go.
I will warm your limbs with kisses
Until they glow.


# *Paradise Re-entered*

Through the strait gate of passion,
Between the bickering fire
Where flames of fierce love tremble
On the body of fierce desire:

To the intoxication,
The mind, fused down like a bead,
Flees in its agitation
The flames' stiff speed:

At last to calm incandescence,
Burned clean by remorseless hate,
Now, at the day's renascence
We approach the gate.

Now, from the darkened spaces
Of fear, and of frightened faces,
Death, in our awed embraces
Approached and passed by;

We near the flame-burnt porches
Where the brands of the angels, like torches,
Whirl,—in these perilous marches
Pausing to sigh;

We look back on the withering roses,
The stars, in their sun-dimmed closes,
Where 'twas given us to repose us
Sure on our sanctity;

Beautiful, candid lovers,
Burnt out of our earthly covers,
We might have nestled like plovers
In the fields of eternity.

There, sure in sinless being,
All-seen, and then all-seeing,
In us life unto death agreeing,
We might have lain.

But we storm the angel-guarded
Gates of the long-discarded
Garden, which God has hoarded
Against our pain.

The Lord of Hosts and the Devil
Are left on Eternity's level
Field, and as victors we travel
To Eden home.

Back beyond good and evil
Return we. Eve dishevel
Your hair for the bliss-drenched revel
On our primal loam.

# *History*

The listless beauty of the hour
When snow fell on the apple-trees
And the wood-ash gathered in the fire
And we faced our first miseries.

Then the sweeping sunshine of noon
When the mountains like chariot cars
Were ranked to blue battle—and you and I
Counted our scars.

And then in a strange, grey hour
We lay mouth to mouth, with your face
Under mine like a star on the lake,
And I covered the earth, and all space.

The silent, drifting hours
Of morn after morn
And night drifting up to the night
Yet no pathway worn.

Your life, and mine, my love
Passing on and on, the hate
Fusing closer and closer with love
Till at length they mate.

*The Cearne.*

# Song of a Man Who Has Come Through

Not I, not I, but the wind that blows through me!
A fine wind is blowing the new direction of Time.
If only I let it bear me, carry me, if only it carry me!
If only I am sensitive, subtle, oh, delicate, a winged gift!
If only, most lovely of all, I yield myself and am borrowed
By the fine, fine wind that takes its course through the chaos
    of the world
Like a fine, an exquisite chisel, a wedge-blade inserted;
If only I am keen and hard like the sheer tip of a wedge
Driven by invisible blows,
The rock will split, we shall come at the wonder, we shall find
    the Hesperides.

Oh, for the wonder that bubbles into my soul,
I would be a good fountain, a good well-head,
Would blur no whisper, spoil no expression.

What is the knocking?
What is the knocking at the door in the night?
It is somebody wants to do us harm.

No, no, it is the three strange angels.
Admit them, admit them.

# THE WORK
# OF CREATION

In these poems, written across his entire career, but particularly in the early 1920s, Lawrence expresses further insights into the sex instinct via other-than-human living things.

# Michael-Angelo

God shook thy roundness in His finger's cup,
He sunk His hands in firmness down thy sides,
And drew the circle of His grasp, O Man,
Along they limbs delighted, thine, His bride's.

And so thou wert God-shapen: His finger
Curved thy mouth for thee, and His strong shoulder
Planted thee upright: art not proud to see
In the curve of thine exquisite form the joy of the Moulder?

He took a handful of light and rolled a ball,
Compressed it till its beam grew wondrous dark,
Then gave thee thy dark eyes, O Man, that all
He made had doorway to thee through that spark.

God, lonely, put down His mouth in a kiss of creation,
He kissed thee, O Man, in a passion of love, and left
The vivid life of His love in thy mouth and thy nostrils;
Keep then the kiss from the adultress' theft.

# Pomegranate

You tell me I am wrong.
Who are you, who is anybody to tell me I am wrong?
I am not wrong.

In Syracuse, rock left bare by the viciousness of Greek women,
No doubt you have forgotten the pomegranate-trees in flower,
Oh so red, and such a lot of them.

Whereas at Venice,
Abhorrent, green, slippery city
Whose Doges were old, and had ancient eyes,
In the dense foliage of the inner garden

Pomegranates like bright green stone,
And barbed, barbed with a crown.
Oh, crown of spiked green metal
Actually growing!

Now in Tuscany,
Pomegranates to warm your hands at;
And crowns, kingly, generous, tilting crowns
Over the left eyebrow.

And if you dare, the fissure!

Do you mean to tell me you will see no fissure?
Do you prefer to look on the plain side?

For all that, the setting suns are open.
The end cracks open with the beginning:
Rosy, tender, glittering within the fissure.

Do you mean to tell me there should be no fissure?
No glittering, compact drops of dawn?
Do you mean it is wrong, the gold-filmed skin, integument,
    shown ruptured?

For my part, I prefer my heart to be broken.
It is so lovely, dawn-kaleidoscopic within the crack.
                              *San Gervasio in Tuscany.*


# *Peach*


Would you like to throw a stone at me?
Here, take all that's left of my peach.

Blood-red, deep;
Heaven knows how it came to pass.
Somebody's pound of flesh rendered up.

Wrinkled with secrets
And hard with the intention to keep them.

Why, from silvery peach-bloom,
From that shallow-silvery wine-glass on a short stem
This rolling, dropping, heavy globule?

I am thinking, of course, of the peach before I ate it.

Why so velvety, why so voluptuous heavy?
Why hanging with such inordinate weight?
Why so indented?

Why the groove?
Why the lovely, bivalve roundnesses?
Why the ripple down the sphere?
Why the suggestion of incision?

Why was not my peach round and finished liked a billiard ball?
It would have been if man had made it.
Though I've eaten it now.

But it wasn't round and finished like a billiard ball.
And because I say so, you would like to throw something at me.

Here, you can have my peach stone.

*San Gervasio.*


# *Purple Anemones*

*Who gave us flowers?*
*Heaven? The white God?*

Nonsense!
Up out of hell,
From Hades;
Infernal Dis!

*Jesus the god of flowers——?*
Not he.
*Or sun-bright Apollo, him so musical?*
Him neither.

*Who then?*
*Say who.*
Say it—and it is Pluto,
Dis,
The dark one.
Proserpine's master.

*Who contradicts——?*

When she broke forth from below,
Flowers came, hell-hounds on her heels.
Dis, the dark, the jealous god, the husband,
Flower-sumptuous-blooded.

*Go then*, he said.
And in Sicily, on the meadows of Enna,
She thought she had left him;
But opened around her purple anemones,
Caverns,
Little hells of colour, caves of darkness,
Hell, risen in pursuit of her; royal, sumptuous
Pit-falls.

All at her feet
Hell opening;
At her white ankles
Hell rearing its husband-splendid, serpent heads,
Hell-purple, to get at her—
*Why did he let her go?*
So he could track her down again, white victim.

Ah mastery!
Hell's husband-blossoms
Out on earth again.

Look out, Persephone!
You, Madame Ceres, mind yourself, the enemy is upon you.
About your feet spontaneous aconite,
Hell-glamorous, and purple husband-tyranny
Enveloping your late-enfranchised plains.

You thought your daughter had escaped?
No more stockings to darn for the flower-roots, down in hell?
But ah, my dear!
Aha, the stripe-cheeked whelps, whippet-slim crocuses,
*At 'em, boys, at 'em!*
*Ho, golden-spaniel, sweet alert narcissus,*
*Smell 'em, smell 'em out!*

Those two enfranchised women.

Somebody is coming!
*Oho there!*
Dark blue anemones!
Hell is up!
Hell on earth, and Dis within the depths!

*Run, Persephone, he is after you already.*

*Why did he let her go?*
To track her down;
All the sport of summer and spring, and flowers snapping at her
    ankles and catching her by the hair!
Poor Persephone and her rights for women.

*Husband-snared hell-queen,*
*It is spring.*

It is spring,
And pomp of husband-strategy on earth.

*Ceres, kiss your girl, you think you've got her back.*
*The bit of husband-tilth she is,*
*Persephone!*

Poor mothers-in-law!
They are always sold.

It is spring.

*Taormina.*

# Snake

A snake came to my water-trough
On a hot, hot day, and I in pyjamas for the heat,
To drink there.

In the deep, strange-scented shade of the great dark carob-tree
I came down the steps with my pitcher
And must wait, must stand and wait, for there he was at the trough
  before me.

He reached down from a fissure in the earth-wall in the gloom
And trailed his yellow-brown slackness soft-bellied down, over the
  edge of the stone trough
And rested his throat upon the stone bottom,
And where the water had dripped from the tap, in a small clearness,
He sipped with his straight mouth,
Softly drank through his straight gums, into his slack long body,
Silently.

Someone was before me at my water-trough,
And I, like a second comer, waiting.

He lifted his head from his drinking, as cattle do,
And looked at me vaguely, as drinking cattle do,
And flickered his two-forked tongue from his lips, and mused a
  moment,
And stooped and drank a little more,
Being earth-brown, earth-golden from the burning bowels of the
  earth
On the day of Sicilian July, with Etna smoking.

The voice of my education said to me
He must be killed,
For in Sicily the black, black snakes are innocent, the gold are
  venomous.

And voices in me said, if you were a man
You would take a stick and break him now, and finish him off.

But must I confess how I liked him,
How glad I was he had come like a guest in quiet, to drink at my
    water-trough
And depart peaceful, pacified, and thankless,
Into the burning bowels of this earth?

Was it cowardice, that I dared not kill him?
Was it perversity, that I longed to talk to him?
Was it humility, to feel so honoured?
I felt so honoured.

And yet those voices:
*If you were not afraid, you would kill him!*

And truly I was afraid, I was most afraid,
But even so, honoured still more
That he should seek my hospitality
From out the dark door of the secret earth.

He drank enough
And lifted his head, dreamily, as one who has drunken,
And flickered his tongue like a forked night on the air, so black,
Seeming to lick his lips,
And looked around like a god, unseeing, into the air,
And slowly turned his head,
And slowly, very slowly, as if thrice adream,
Proceeded to draw his slow length curving round
And climb again the broken bank of my wall-face.

And as he put his head into that dreadful hole,
And as he slowly drew up, snake-easing his shoulders, and entered
    farther,
A sort of horror, a sort of protest against his withdrawing into that
    horrid black hole,
Deliberately going into the blackness, and slowly drawing himself
    after,
Overcame me now his back was turned.

I looked round, I put down my pitcher,
I picked up a clumsy log
And threw it at the water-trough with a clatter.

I think it did not hit him,
But suddenly that part of him that was left behind convulsed in
     undignified haste,
Writhed like lightning, and was gone
Into the black hole, the earth-lipped fissure in the wall-front,
At which, in the intense still noon, I stared with fascination.

And immediately I regretted it.
I thought how paltry, how vulgar, what a mean act!
I despised myself and the voices of my accursed human education.

And I thought of the albatross,
And I wished he would come back, my snake.

For he seemed to me again like a king,
Like a king in exile, uncrowned in the underworld,
Now due to be crowned again.

And so, I missed my chance with one of the lords
Of life.
And I have something to expiate;
A pettiness.

                              *Taormina.*


# *Tortoise Family Connections*

On he goes, the little one,
Bud of the universe,
Pediment of life.

Setting off somewhere, apparently.
Whither away, brisk egg?

His mother deposited him on the soil as if he were no more than
    droppings,
And now he scuffles tinily past her as if she were an old rusty tin.

A mere obstacle,
He veers round the slow great mound of her—
Tortoises always foresee obstacles.
It is no use my saying to him in an emotional voice:
'This is your Mother, she laid you when you were an egg.'

He does not even trouble to answer: 'Woman, what have I to do
    with thee?'
He wearily looks the other way,
And she even more wearily looks another way still,
Each with the utmost apathy,
Incognisant,
Unaware,
Nothing.

As for papa,
He snaps when I offer him his offspring,
Just as he snaps when I poke a bit of stick at him,
Because he is irascible this morning, an irascible tortoise
Being touched with love, and devoid of fatherliness.

Father and mother,
And three little brothers,
And all rambling aimless, like little perambulating pebbles scattered
    in the garden,
Not knowing each other from bits of earth or old tins.

Except that papa and mama are old acquaintances, of course,
Though family feeling there is none, not even the beginnings.

Fatherless, motherless, brotherless, sisterless
Little tortoise.

Row on then, small pebble,
Over the clods of the autumn, wind-chilled sunshine,
Young gaiety.

Does he look for a companion?

No, no, don't think it.
He doesn't know he is alone;
Isolation is his birthright,
This atom.

To row forward, and reach himself tall on spiny toes,
To travel, to burrow into a little loose earth, afraid of the night,
To crop a little substance,
To move, and to be quite sure that he is moving:
Basta!
To be a tortoise!
Think of it, in a garden of inert clods
A brisk, brindled little tortoise, all to himself—
Adam!

In a garden of pebbles and insects
To roam, and feel the slow heart beat
Tortoise-wise, the first bell sounding
From the warm blood, in the dark-creation morning.

Moving, and being himself,
Slow, and unquestioned,
And inordinately there, O stoic!
Wandering in the slow triumph of his own existence,
Ringing the soundless bell of his presence in chaos,
And biting the frail grass arrogantly,
Decidedly arrogantly.

## *Tortoise Shout*

I thought he was dumb,
I said he was dumb,
Yet I've heard him cry.

First faint scream,
Out of life's unfathomable dawn,
Far off, so far, like a madness, under the horizon's dawning rim,
Far, far off, far scream.

Tortoise *in extremis.*

Why were we crucified into sex?
Why were we not left rounded off, and finished in ourselves,
As we began,
As he certainly began, so perfectly alone?

A far, was-it-audible scream,
Or did it sound on the plasm direct?

Worse than the cry of the new-born,
A scream,
A yell,
A shout,
A pæan,
A death-agony,
A birth-cry,
A submission,
All tiny, tiny, far away, reptile under the first dawn.

War-cry, triumph, acute-delight, death-scream reptilian,
Why was the veil torn?
The silken shriek of the soul's torn membrane?
The male soul's membrane
Torn with a shriek half music, half horror.

Crucifixion.
Male tortoise, cleaving behind the hovel-wall of that dense female,
Mounted and tense, spread-eagle, out-reaching out of the shell
In tortoise-nakedness,
Long neck, and long vulnerable limbs extruded, spread-eagle over
    her house-roof,
And the deep, secret, all-penetrating tail curved beneath her walls,
Reaching and gripping tense, more reaching anguish in uttermost
    tension

Till suddenly, in the spasm of coition, tupping like a jerking leap,
    and oh!
Opening its clenched face from his outstretched neck
And giving that fragile yell, that scream,
Super-audible,
From his pink, cleft, old-man's mouth,
Giving up the ghost,
Or screaming in Pentecost, receiving the ghost.

His scream, and his moment's subsidence,
The moment of eternal silence,
Yet unreleased, and after the moment, the sudden, startling jerk of
    coition, and at once
The inexpressible faint yell—
And so on, till the last plasm of my body was melted back
To the primeval rudiments of life, and the secret.

So he tups, and screams
Time after time that frail, torn scream
After each jerk, the longish interval,
The tortoise eternity,
Age-long, reptilian persistence,
Heart-throb, slow heart-throb, persistent for the next spasm.

I remember, when I was a boy,
I heard the scream of a frog, which was caught with his foot in the
    mouth of an up-starting snake;
I remember when I first heard bull-frogs break into sound in the
    spring;
I remember hearing a wild goose out of the throat of night
Cry loudly, beyond the lake of waters;
I remember the first time, out of a bush in the darkness, a
    nightingale's piercing cries and gurgles startled the depths of my
    soul;
I remember the scream of a rabbit, as I went through a wood at
    midnight;
I remember the heifer in her heat, blorting and blorting through the
    hours, persistent and irrepressible;

I remember my first terror hearing the howl of weird, amorous cats;
I remember the scream of a terrified, injured horse, the sheet-
　　lightning,
And running away from the sound of a woman in labour, something
　　like an owl whooing,
And listening inwardly to the first bleat of a lamb,
The first wail of an infant,
And my mother singing to herself,
And the first tenor singing of the passionate throat of a young
　　collier, who has long since drunk himself to death,
The first elements of foreign speech
On wild dark lips.

And more than all these,
And less than all these,
This last,
Strange, faint coition yell
Of the male tortoise at extremity,
Tiny from under the very edge of the farthest far-off horizon of life.

The cross,
The wheel on which our silence first is broken,
Sex, which breaks up our integrity, our single inviolability, our deep
　　silence,
Tearing a cry from us.

Sex, which breaks us into voice, sets us calling across the deeps,
　　calling, calling for the complement,
Singing, and calling, and singing again, being answered, having
　　found.

Torn, to become whole again, after long seeking for what is lost,
The same cry from the tortoise as from Christ, the Osiris-cry of
　　abandonment,
That which is whole, torn asunder,
That which is in part, finding its whole again throughout the
　　universe.

# The Ass

The long-drawn bray of the ass
In the Sicilian twilight—

*All mares are dead!*
*All mares are dead!*
*Oh-h!*
*Oh-h-h!*
*Oh-h-h-h-h—h!!*
*I can't bear it, I can't bear it.*
*I can't!*
*Oh, I can't!*
*Oh—*
*There's one left!*
*There's one left!*
*One!*
*There's one ... left....*
So ending on a grunt of agonised relief.

This is the authentic Arabic interpretation of the braying of the ass.
And Arabs should know.

And yet, as his brass-resonant howling yell resounds through the
    Sicilian twilight
I am not sure—

His big, furry head,
His big, regretful eyes,
His diminished, drooping hindquarters,
His small toes.

Such a dear!
Such an ass!
With such a knot inside him!
He regrets something that he remembers.
That's obvious.

The Steppes of Tartary,
And the wind in his teeth for a bit,
And *noli me tangere*.

Ah then, when he tore the wind with his teeth,
And trod wolves underfoot,
And over-rode his mares as if he were savagely leaping an obstacle,
    to set his teeth in the sun. . . .

Somehow, alas, he fell in love,
And was sold into slavery.

He fell into the rut of love,
Poor ass, like man, always in rut,
The pair of them alike in that.

All his soul in his gallant member
And his head gone heavy with the knowledge of desire
And humiliation.

The ass was the first of all animals to fall finally into love,
From obstacle-leaping pride,
Mare obstacle,
Into-love, mare-goal, and the knowledge of love.

Hence Jesus rode him in the Triumphant Entry.
Hence his beautiful eyes.
Hence his ponderous head, brooding over desire, and downfall, Jesus,
    and a pack-saddle,
Hence he uncovers his big ass-teeth and howls in that agony that is
    half insatiable desire and half unquenchable humiliation.
Hence the black cross on his shoulders.

The Arabs were only half right, though they hinted the whole;
Everlasting lament in everlasting desire.

See him standing with his head down, near the Porta Cappuccini,
Asinello, Ciuco,
Somaro;
With the half-veiled, beautiful eyes, and the pensive face not asleep,
Motionless, like a bit of rock.

Has he seen the Gorgon's head, and turned to stone?
Alas, Love did it.
Now he's a jackass, a pack-ass, a donkey, somaro, burro, with a boss
   piling loads on his back.
Tied by the nose at the Porta Cappuccini.
And tied in a knot, inside, dead-locked between two desires:
To overlap like a male all mares as obstacles
In a leap at the sun;
And to leap in one last heart-bursting leap like a male at the goal of
   a mare.
And there end.
Well, you can't have it both roads.

*Hee! Hee! Ehee! Ehow! Ehaw!! Oh! Oh! Oh-h-h!!*
The wave of agony bursts in the stone that he was,
Bares his long ass's teeth, flattens his long ass's ears, straightens his
   donkey neck,
And howls his pandemonium on the indignant air.
Yes, it's a quandary.
Jesus rode on him, the first burden on the first beast of burden.
Love on a submissive ass.
So the tale began.

But the ass never forgets.

The horse, being nothing but a nag, will forget.
And men, being mostly geldings and knacker-boned hacks, have
   almost all forgot.
But the ass is a primal creature, and never forgets.

The Steppes of Tartary,
And Jesus on a meek ass-colt: mares: Mary escaping to Egypt:
   Joseph's cudgel.

*Hee! Hee! Ehee! Ehow-ow!-ow!-aw!-aw!-aw!*
*All mares are dead!*

*Or else I am dead!*
*One of us, or the pair of us,*
*I don't know–ow!–ow!*
*Which!*
*Not sure–ure–ure*
*Quite which!*
*Which!*

                                        *Taormina.*

# She-Goat

Goats go past the back of the house like dry leaves in the dawn,
And up the hill like a river, if you watch.
At dusk they patter back like a bough being dragged on the ground,
Raising dusk and acridity of goats, and bleating.

Our old goat we tie up at night in the shed at the back of the broken
    Greek tomb in the garden,
And when the herd goes by at dawn she begins to bleat for me to
    come down and untie her.

*Merr–err–err! Merr–er–errr! Mer! Mé!*
*—Wait, wait a bit, I'll come when I've lit the fire.*
*Merrr!*
*—Exactly.*
*Mé! Mer! Merrrrrr!!!*
*—Tace, tu, crapa, bestia!*
*Merr–ererrr–ererrr! Merrrr!*

She is such an alert listener, with her ears wide, to know am I
    coming!
Such a canny listener, from a distance, looking upwards, lending first
    one ear, then another.

There she is, perched on her manger, looking over the boards into
    the day
Like a belle at her window.
And immediately she sees me she blinks, stares, doesn't know me,
    turns her head and ignores me vulgarly with a wooden blank on
    her face.

What do I care for her, the ugly female, standing up there with her
    long tangled sides like an old rug thrown over a fence.
But she puts her nose down shrewdly enough when the knot is
    untied,
And jumps staccato to earth, a sharp, dry jump, still ignoring me,
Pretending to look round the stall.

*Come on, you, crapa! I'm not your servant!*

She turns her head away with an obtuse, female sort of deafness,
    bête.
And then invariably she crouches her rear and makes water.
That being her way of answer, if I speak to her.—Self-conscious!
*Le bestie non parlano, poverine!*

She was bought at Giardini fair, on the sands, for six hundred lire.

An obstinate old witch, almost jerking the rope from my hands to
    eat the acanthus, or bite at the almond buds, and make me wait.
Yet the moment I hate her she trips mild and smug like a woman
    going to mass.
The moment I really detest her.

Queer it is, suddenly, in the garden
To catch sight of her standing like some huge, ghoulish grey bird in
    the air, on the bough of the leaning almond-tree,
Straight as a board on the bough, looking down like some hairy
    horrid God the Father in a William Blake imagination.
*Come down, crapa, out of that almond-tree!*

Instead of which she strangely rears on her perch in the air,
    vast beast,
And strangely paws the air, delicate,
And reaches her black-striped face up like a snake, far up,
Subtly, to the twigs overhead, far up, vast beast,
And snaps them sharp, with a little twist of her anaconda head;
All her great hairy-shaggy belly open against the morning.

At seasons she curls back her tail like a green leaf in the fire,
Or like a lifted hand, hailing at her wrong end.
And having exposed the pink place of her nakedness, fixedly,
She trots on blithe toes,
And if you look at her, she looks back with a cold, sardonic stare.
Sardonic, sardonyx, rock of cold fire.
*See me?* She says, *That's me!*

That's her.

Then she leaps the rocks like a quick rock,
Her backbone sharp as a rock,
Sheer will.

Along which ridge of libidinous magnetism
Defiant, curling the leaf of her tail as if she were curling her lip
    behind her at all life,
Libidinous desire runs back and forth, asserting itself in that little
    lifted bare hand.

Yet she has such adorable spurty kids, like spurts of black ink.
And in a month again is as if she had never had them.

And when the billy goat mounts her
She is brittle as brimstone.
While his slitted eyes squint back to the roots of his ears.
                              *Taormina.*

# *Fish*

Fish, oh Fish,
So little matters!

Whether the waters rise and cover the earth
Or whether the waters wilt in the hollow places,
All one to you.

Aqueous, subaqueous,
Submerged
And wave-thrilled.

As the waters roll
Roll you.
The waters wash,
You wash in oneness
And never emerge.

Never know,
Never grasp.

Your life a sluice of sensation along your sides,
A flush at the flails of your fins, down the whorl of your tail,
And water wetly on fire in the grates of your gills;
Fixed water-eyes.

Even snakes lie together.

But oh, fish, that rock in water,
You lie only with the waters;
One touch.

No fingers, no hands and feet, no lips;
No tender muzzles,
No wistful bellies,
No loins of desire,
None.

You and the naked element,
Sway-wave.
Curvetting bits of tin in the evening light.

Who is it ejects his sperm to the naked flood?
In the wave-mother?
Who swims enwombed?
Who lies with the waters of his silent passion, womb-element?
—Fish in the waters under the earth.

What price *his* bread upon the waters?

Himself all silvery himself
In the element,
No more.

Nothing more.

Himself,
And the element.
Food, of course!
Water-eager eyes,
Mouth-gate open
And strong spine urging, driving;
And desirous belly gulping.

Fear also!
He knows fear!
Water-eyes craning,
A rush that almost screams,
Almost fish-voice
As the pike comes. . . .
Then gay fear, that turns the tail sprightly, from a shadow.

Food, and fear, and joie de vivre,
Without love.

The other way about:
Joie de vivre, and fear, and food,
All without love.

Quelle joie de vivre
Dans l'eau!
Slowly to gape through the waters,
Alone with the element;
To sink, and rise, and go to sleep with the waters;
To speak endless inaudible wavelets into the wave;
To breathe from the flood at the gills,
Fish-blood slowly running next to the flood, extracting fish-fire:
To have the element under one, like a lover;
And to spring away with a curvetting click in the air,
Provocative.
Dropping back with a slap on the face of the flood.
And merging oneself!

To be a fish!

So utterly without misgiving
To be a fish
In the waters.

Loveless, and so lively!
Born before God was love,
Or life knew loving.
Beautifully beforehand with it all.

Admitted, they swarm in companies,
Fishes.
They drive in shoals.
But soundless, and out of contact.
They exchange no word, no spasm, not even anger.
Not one touch.
Many suspended together, forever apart,
Each one alone with the waters, upon one wave with the rest.

A magnetism in the water between them only.

I saw a water-serpent swim across the Anapo,
And I said to my heart, *look, look at him!*
*With his head up, steering like a bird!*
*He's a rare one, but he belongs . . .*

But sitting in a boat on the Zeller lake
And watching the fishes in the breathing waters
Lift and swim and go their way—

I said to my heart, *who are these?*
And my heart couldn't own them. . . .

A slim young pike, with smart fins
And grey-striped suit, a young cub of a pike
Slouching along away below, half out of sight,
Like a lout on an obscure pavement. . . .

Aha, there's somebody in the know!

But watching closer
That motionless deadly motion,
That unnatural barrel body, that long, ghoul nose. . . .
I left off hailing him.

I had made a mistake, I didn't know him,
This grey, monotonous soul in the water,
This intense individual in shadow,
Fish-alive.

I didn't know his God,
I didn't know his God.

Which is perhaps the last admission that life has to wring out of us.

I saw, dimly,
Once a big pike rush,
And small fish fly like splinters.
And I said to my heart, *there are limits*
*To you, my heart;*
*And to the one God.*
*Fish are beyond me.*

Other Gods
Beyond my range . . . gods beyond my God. . . .

They are beyond me, are fishes.
I stand at the pale of my being
And look beyond, and see
Fish, in the outerwards,
As one stands on a bank and looks in.

I have waited with a long rod
And suddenly pulled a gold-and-greenish, lucent fish from below,
And had him fly like a halo round my head,
Lunging in the air on the line.

Unhooked his gorping, water-horny mouth,
And seen his horror-tilted eye,
His red-gold, water-precious, mirror-flat bright eye;
And felt him beat in my hand, with his mucous, leaping life-throb.
And my heart accused itself
Thinking: *I am not the measure of creation.*
*This is beyond me, this fish.*
*His God stands outside my God.*

And the gold-and-green pure lacquer-mucus comes off in my hand,
And the red-gold mirror-eye stares and dies,
And the water-suave contour dims.

But not before I have had to know
He was born in front of my sunrise,
Before my day.

He outstarts me.
And I, a many-fingered horror of daylight to him,
Have made him die.

Fishes
With their gold, red eyes, and green-pure gleam, and under-gold,
And their pre-world loneliness,
And more-than-lovelessness,
And white meat;
They move in other circles.

Outsiders.
Water-wayfarers.
Things of one element.
Aqueous,
Each by itself.

Cats, and the Neapolitans,
Sulphur sub-beasts,
Thirst for fish as for more-than-water;
Water-alive
To quench their over-sulphureous lusts.

But I, I only wonder
And don't know
I don't know fishes.

In the beginning
Jesus was called The Fish. . . .
And in the end.

*Zell-am-See.*

# Mountain Lion

Climbing through the January snow, into the Lobo canyon
Dark grow the spruce-trees, blue is the balsam, water sounds still
    unfrozen, and the trail is still evident.

Men!
Two men!
Men! The only animal in the world to fear!

They hesitate.
We hesitate.
They have a gun.
We have no gun.

Then we all advance, to meet.

Two Mexicans, strangers, emerging out of the dark and snow and
    inwardness of the Lobo valley.
What are they doing here on this vanishing trail?

What is he carrying?
Something yellow.
A deer?

*Qué tiene, amigo?*
*León—*

He smiles, foolishly, as if he were caught doing wrong.
And we smile, foolishly, as if we didn't know.
He is quite gentle and dark-faced.

It is a mountain lion,
A long, long slim cat, yellow like a lioness.
Dead.

He trapped her this morning, he says, smiling foolishly.

Lift up her face,
Her round, bright face, bright as frost.
Her round, fine-fashioned head, with two dead ears;
And stripes in the brilliant frost of her face, sharp, fine dark rays,
Dark, keen, fine rays in the brilliant frost of her face.
Beautiful dead eyes.

*Hermoso es!*

They go out towards the open;
We go on into the gloom of Lobo.
And above the trees I found her lair,
A hole in the blood-orange brilliant rocks that stick up, a little cave,
And bones, and twigs, and a perilous ascent.

So, she will never leap up that way again, with the yellow flash of a
    mountain lion's long shoot!
And her bright striped frost-face will never watch any more, out of
    the shadow of the cave in the blood-orange rock,
Above the trees of the Lobo dark valley-mouth!

Instead, I look out.

And out to the dim of the desert, like a dream, never real;

To the snow of the Sangre de Cristo mountains, the ice of the
mountains of Picoris,

And near across at the opposite steep of snow, green trees
motionless standing in snow, like a Christmas toy.

And I think in this empty world there was room for me and a
mountain lion.

And I think in the world beyond, how easily we might spare a
million or two of humans

And never miss them.

Yet what a gap in the world, the missing white frost-face of that
slim yellow mountain lion!

*Lobo.*

# *The Elephant is Slow to Mate*

The elephant, the huge old beast,
    is slow to mate;
he finds a female, they show no haste
    they wait

for the sympathy in their vast shy hearts
    slowly, slowly to rouse
as they loiter along the river-beds
    and drink and browse

and dash in panic through the brake
    of forest with the herd,
and sleep in massive silence, and wake
    together, without a word.

So slowly the great hot elephant hearts
    grow full of desire,
and the great beasts mate in secret at last,
    hiding their fire.

Oldest they are and the wisest of beasts
  so they know at last
how to wait for the loneliest of feasts
  for the full repast.

They do not snatch, they do not tear;
  their massive blood
moves as the moon-tides, near, more near,
  till they touch in flood.

# *[Flat-foot's Song]*

Because Flat-foot is the favourite of the white leghorn cock, and he shakes the tid-bit for her with a most wooing noise, and when she lays an egg, he bristles like a double white poppy, and rushes to meet her, as she flounders down from the chicken-house, and his echo of her *I've-laid-an-egg* cackle is rich and resonant. Every pine-tree on the mountains hears him:

    She's }
    I've }   *laid an egg!*
    She's }
    I've }   *laid an egg!*

And his poem would be:

  'Oh you who made me feel so good, when
    you sit next me on the perch
  At night! (temporarily, of course!)
  Oh you who make my feathers bristle with
    the vanity of life!
  Oh you whose cackle makes my throat go
    off like a rocket!
  Oh you who walk so slowly, and make me
    feel swifter
  Than my boss!
  Oh you who bend your head down, and

> move in the under
> Circle, while I prance in the upper!
> Oh you, come! come! come! for here is a bit
>    of fat from
> The roast veal; I am shaking it for you.'

# *Whales Weep Not!*

They say the sea is cold, but the sea contains
The hottest blood of all, and the wildest, the most urgent.

All the whales in the wider deeps, hot are they, as they urge
on and on, and dive beneath the icebergs.
The right whales, the sperm-whales, the hammer-heads, the killers
   there they blow, there they blow, hot wild white breath out of the
   sea!

And they rock, and they rock, through the sensual ageless ages
on the depths of the seven seas,
and through the salt they reel with drunk delight
and in the tropics tremble they with love
and roll with massive, strong desire, like gods.
Then the great bull lies up against his bride
in the blue deep bed of the sea,
as mountain pressing on mountain, in the zest of life:
and out of the inward roaring of the inner red ocean of whale-blood
   the long tip reaches strong, intense, like the maelstrom-tip, and
   comes to rest
in the clasp and the soft, wild clutch of a she-whale's fathomless
   body.

And over the bridge of the whale's strong phallus, linking the
   wonder of whales
the burning archangels under the sea keep passing, back and forth,
   keep passing, archangels of bliss
from him to her, from her to him, great Cherubim
that wait on whales in mid-ocean, suspended in the waves of the sea

great heaven of whales in the waters, old hierarchies.
And enormous mother whales lie dreaming suckling their whale-
tender young
and dreaming with strange whale eyes wide open in the waters of
the beginning and the end.
And bull-whales gather their women and whale-calves in a ring
when danger threatens, on the surface of the ceaseless flood
and range themselves like great fierce Seraphim facing the threat
encircling their huddled monsters of love.
And all this happens in the sea, in the salt
where God is also love, but without words:
and Aphrodite is the wife of whales
most happy, happy she!

and Venus among the fishes skips and is a she-dolphin
she is the gay, delighted porpoise sporting with love and the sea
she is the female tunny-fish, round and happy among the males
and dense with happy blood, dark rainbow bliss in the sea.

# LYRICS, PROFFERED WISDOMS AND SATIRES

Moments of joy and opinions about how life should be lived, how love should really be felt, and sex; along with sarcasms about those who remain in emotional or sexual ignorance. Many of these poems come from Lawrence's 1929 volume *Pansies*.

# LYRICS

## *Gipsy*

I, the man with the red scarf,
  Will give thee what I have, this last week's earnings
Take them and buy thee a silver ring
  And wed me, to ease my yearnings.

For the rest, when thou art wedded
  I'll wet my brow for thee
With sweat, I'll enter a house for thy sake,
  Thou shalt shut doors on me.

Between thy moon-lit, milk-white thighs
  Is a moon-pool in thee.
And the sun in me is thirsty, it cries
  To drink thee, to win thee.

I am black with the sun, and willing
  To be dead
Can I but plunge in thee, swilling
  Thy waves over my head.

## *[Unfortunate Interrupted Lovers]*

'Quick, sharp, on the alert
Let every gentleman put on his shirt!
And, oh, quick if you please
Let every lady get on her chemise!'

# Leda

Come not with kisses
not with caresses
of hands and lips and murmurings;
come with a hiss of wings
and sea-touch tip of a beak
and treading of wet, webbed, wave-working feet
into the marsh-soft belly.

# Little Fish

The tiny fish enjoy themselves
in the sea.
Quick little splinters of life,
their little lives are fun to them
in the sea.

# Spray

It is a wonder foam is so beautiful.
A wave bursts in anger on a rock, broken up
in wild white sibilant spray
and falls back, drawing in its breath with rage,
with frustration how beautiful!

# Sea-weed

Sea-weed sways and sways and swirls
as if swaying were its form of stillness;
and if it flushes against fierce rock
it slips over it as shadows do, without hurting itself.

# They Say the Sea is Loveless

They say the sea is loveless, that in the sea
love cannot live, but only bare, salt splinters
of loveless life.

But from the sea
the dolphins leap round Dionysos' ship
whose masts have purple vines,
and up they come with the purple dark of rainbows
and flip! they go! with the nose-dive of sheer delight;
and the sea is making love to Dionysos
in the bouncing of these small and happy whales.

# You

You, you don't know me.
When have your knees ever nipped me
like fire-tongs a live coal
for a minute?

# Three Poems in Wartime

## Maiden's Prayer

I have come to the house of God
And found grey doves in the fountain court
Feeding on pure white sugar
Curving their feet and dancing and fluttering in sport.

I wish I could have some too
Some sugar of the same white sort
And let them feed from my hand.—
But alas, this is not what I came for! I have fallen short.

*Lord, cherish and comfort*
*The man Andrew; keep him safe in the war*
*From falling iron and horrible shells' report.*
*And Lord*—But hark at the pigeons, what are they clattering for?


## Swing Song of a Girl and a Soldier

Brother, the scent of your clothing
Is like biscuits baked for a feast
Of victory, kneaded with sulphur
Worked with clean sweat for yeast.

Brother, I like your fragrance.
It smells strange like the shouting of men
Womanless shouting in anger.
Brother, let me die down again.


## The Jewess and the V.C.

Ah, young man
What sort of timorous potion of love have you drunk?
   If you see my rings, how they sparkle within my ears,
You go about in a dream, with your countenance sunk,
   And children behind you taunting you to tears.

Why, if you saw my limbs, how they shine on my body,
   What then would you do? Then for sure you would go
And die like a dog in a hole. 'Tis strange what a shoddy
   Lover you make, such a hero in front of the foe!

# PROFFERED WISDOMS

## Rainbow

One thing that is bow-legged
and can't put its feet together
is the rainbow.
Even if the Lord God shouted
—Attention!—
it couldn't put its feet together.

Yet it's got two feet
as you know,
and two pots of gold
we are told.

What I see
when I look at the rainbow
is one foot in the lap of a woman
and one in the loins of a man.

The feet of the arch
that the Lord God rested the worlds on.

And wide, wide apart,
with nothing but desire between them.

The two feet of the rainbow
want to put themselves together.
But they can't, or there'd be the vicious circle.

So they leap up like a fountain.
He leaps up, she leaps up,
like rockets!
and they curve over.

From the heart a red ray,
from the brow a gold,
from the hips a violet
leaps.

Dark blue the whole desire leaps
brindled with rays
all of the colours
that leap

and lean over
in the arch
of the rainbow.

They will always do it.
The Lord God said so.

If there are pots of gold
they are pails
of the honey of experience
hanging from the shoulders of the rainbow.

But the one thing that is bow-legged
and can't put its feet together
is the rainbow.

Because one foot is the heart of a man
and the other is the heart of a woman.
And these two, as you know,
never meet.

Save they leap
high—
Oh hearts, leap high!
—they touch in mid-heaven like an acrobat
and make a rainbow.

## We are Transmitters

As we live, we are transmitters of life.
And when we fail to transmit life, life fails to flow through us.

That is part of the mystery of sex, it is a flow onwards.
Sexless people transmit nothing.

And if, as we work, we can transmit life into our work,
life, still more life, rushes into us to compensate, to be ready
and we ripple with life through the days.

Even if it is a woman making an apple dumpling, or a man a stool,
if life goes into the pudding, good is the pudding,
good is the stool,
content is the woman, with fresh life rippling in her,
content is the man.

Give, and it shall be given unto you
is still the truth about life.

But giving life is not so easy.

It doesn't mean handing it out to some mean fool, or letting the
    living dead eat you up.

It means kindling the life-quality where it was not,
even if it's only in the whiteness of a washed pocket-handkerchief.

# *Sex Isn't Sin*

Sex isn't sin, ah no! sex isn't sin,
nor is it dirty, not until the dirty mind pokes in.

We shall do as we like, sin is obsolete, the young assert.
Sin is obsolete, sin is obsolete, but not so dirt.

And sex, alas, gets dirtier and dirtier, worked from the mind.
Sex gets dirtier and dirtier, the more it is fooled with, we find.

And dirt, if it isn't sin, is worse, especially dirt inside.
If you're dirty inside you go rotten, and once rotten, woe betide!

Sex isn't sin, but dirty sex is worse, so there you are!
Why don't you know what's what, young people? Seems to me
you're far duller than your grandmothers. But leave that aside.
Let's be honest at last about sex, or show at least that we've tried.

Sex isn't sin, it's a delicate flow between women and men,
and the sin is to damage the flow, force it or dirty it or suppress it
    again.

Sex isn't something you've got to play with; sex is *you*.
It's the flow of your life, it's your moving self, and you are due
to be true to the nature of it, its reserve, its sensitive pride
that it always has to begin with, and by which you ought to abide.

Know yourself, O know yourself, that you are mortal; and know
the sensitive delicacy of your sex, in its ebbing to and fro,
and the mortal reserve of your sex, as it stays in your depths below.

And don't, with the nasty, prying mind, drag it out from its deeps
and finger it and force it, and shatter the rhythm it keeps
when it's left alone, as it stirs and rouses and sleeps.

O know yourself, O know your sex! You must know, there is no
    escape.
You must know sex in order to save it, your deepest self, from the
    rape
of the itching mind and the mental self, with its pruriency always
    agape.


# In a Spanish Tram-car

She fanned herself with a violet fan
and looked sulky, under her thick straight brows.

The wisp of modern black mantilla
made her half Madonna, half Astarte.

Suddenly her yellow-brown eyes looked with a flare into mine;
—We could sin together!—

The spark fell and kindled instantly on my blood,
then died out almost as swiftly.

She can keep her sin
She can sin with some thick-set Spaniard.
Sin doesn't interest me.

# The Mess of Love

We've made a great mess of love
since we made an ideal of it.

The moment I swear to love a woman, a certain woman, all my life
that moment I begin to hate her.

The moment I even say to a woman: I love you!—
my love dies down considerably.

The moment love is an understood thing between us, we are sure of
    it,
it's a cold egg, it isn't love any more.
Love is like a flower, it must flower and fade;
if it doesn't fade, it is not a flower,
it's either an artificial rag blossom, or an immortelle, for the
    cemetery.

The moment the mind interferes with love, or the will fixes on it,
or the personality assumes it as an attribute, or the ego takes
    possession of it,
it is not love any more, it's just a mess.
And we've made a great mess of love, mind-perverted, will-
    perverted, ego-perverted love.

# The Effort of Love

I am worn out
with the effort of trying to love people
and not succeeding.

Now I've made up my mind
I love nobody, I'm going to love nobody,
I'm not going to tell any lies about it
and it's final.

If there's a man here and there, or a woman
whom I can really like,
that's quite enough for me.

And if by a miracle a woman happened to come along
who warmed the cockles of my heart
I'd rejoice over the woman and the warmed cockles of my heart
so long as it didn't all fizzle out in talk.

## *Chastity*

Chastity, beloved chastity
O beloved chastity
how infinitely dear to me
chastity, beloved chastity!

That my body need not be
fingered by the mind,
or prostituted by the dree
contact of cerebral flesh—

O leave me clean from mental fingering
from the cold copulation of the will,
from all the white, self-conscious lechery
the modern mind calls love!

From all the mental poetry
of deliberate love-making,
from all the false felicity
of deliberately taking

the body of another unto mine,
O God deliver me!
leave me alone, let me be!
Chastity, dearer far to me

than any contact that can be
in this mind-mischievous age!

# Lies About Love

We are all liars, because
the truth of yesterday becomes a lie tomorrow,
whereas letters are fixed,
and we live by the letter of truth.

The love I feel for my friend, this year,
is different from the love I felt last year.
If it were not so, it would be a lie.
Yet we reiterate love! love!
as if it were coin with a fixed value
instead of a flower that dies, and opens a different bud.

# Retort to Jesus

And whoever forces himself to love anybody
begets a murderer in his own body.

# Commandments

When Jesus commanded us to love our neighbour
he forced us either to live a great lie, or to disobey:
for we can't love anybody, neighbour or no neighbour, to order,
and faked love has rotted our marrow.

# Glimpses

What's the good of a man
unless there's the glimpse of a god in him?
And what's the good of a woman
unless she's a glimpse of a goddess of some sort?

# For a Moment

For a moment, at evening, tired, as he stepped off the tram-car,
—the young tram-conductor in a blue uniform, to himself
    forgotten,—
and lifted his face up, with blue eyes looking at the electric rod
    which he was going to turn round,
for a moment, pure in the yellow evening light, he was Hyacinthus.

In the green garden darkened the shadow of coming rain
and a girl ran swiftly, laughing breathless, taking in her white
    washing
in rapid armfuls from the line, tossing it in the basket,
and so rapidly, and so flashing, fleeing before the rain
for a moment she was Io, Io, who fled from Zeus, or the Danaë.

When I was waiting and not thinking, sitting at a table on the hotel
    terrace
I saw suddenly coming towards me, lit up and uplifted with pleasure
advancing with the slow-swiftness of a ship backing her white sails
    into port
the woman who looks for me in the world
and for the moment she was Isis, gleaming, having found her Osiris.

For a moment, as he looked at me through his spectacles
pondering, yet eager, the broad and thick-set Italian who works in
    with me,
for a moment he was the Centaur, the wise yet horse-hoofed
Centaur in whom I can trust.

# The Man of Tyre

The man of Tyre went down to the sea
pondering, for he was Greek, that God is one and all alone and ever
    more shall be so.
And a woman who had been washing clothes in the pool of rock

where a stream came down to the gravel of the sea and sank in,
who had spread white washing on the gravel banked above the bay,
who had lain her shift on the shore, on the shingle slope,
who had waded to the pale green sea of evening out to a shoal,
pouring sea-water over herself
now turned, and came slowly back, with her back to the evening sky.

Oh lovely, lovely with the dark hair piled up, as she went deeper,
    deeper down the channel, then rose shallower, shallower,
with the full thighs slowly lifting of the wader wading shorewards
and the shoulders pallid with light from the silent sky behind both
breasts dim and mysterious, with the glamorous kindness of twilight
    between them
and the dim blotch of black maidenhair like an indicator,
giving a message to the man—

So in the cane-brake he clasped his hands in delight
that could only be god-given, and murmured:
Lo! God is one god! But here in the twilight
godly and lovely comes Aphrodite out of the sea
towards me!


# To Women, as Far as I'm Concerned

The feelings I don't have I don't have.
The feelings I don't have I won't say I have.
The feelings you say you have, you don't have.
The feelings you would like us both to have, we neither of us have.

The feelings people ought to have, they never have.
If people say they've got feelings, you may be pretty sure they
    haven't got them.

So if you want either of us to feel anything at all
you'd better abandon all idea of feelings altogether.

# *SATIRES*

## *All-knowing*

All that we know is nothing, we are merely crammed waste-paper
   baskets
unless we are in touch with that which laughs at all our knowing.

## *When I Went to the Film*

When I went to the film, and saw all the black-and-white
   feelings that nobody felt,
and heard the audience sighing and sobbing with all the
   emotions they none of them felt,
and saw them cuddling with rising passions they none of
   them for a moment felt
and caught them moaning from close-up kisses, black-and-
   white kisses that could not be felt,
It was like being in heaven, which I am sure has a white
   atmosphere
upon which shadows of people, pure personalities
are cast in black and white, and move
in flat ecstasy, supremely unfelt,
and heavenly.

## *Film Passion*

If all those females who so passionately loved
the film face of Rudolf Valentino
had had to take him for one night only, in the flesh,
how they'd have hated him!

Hated him just because he was a man
and flesh of a man.
For the luscious filmy imagination loathes the male
    substance with deadly loathing.

All the women who adored the shadow of the man on
    the screen
helped to kill him in the flesh.
Such adoration pierces the loins and perishes the man
worse than the evil eye.

# No! Mr Lawrence!

No, Mr. Lawrence, it's not like that!
I don't mind telling you
I know a thing or two about love,
perhaps more than you do.

And what I know is that you make it
too nice, too beautiful.
It's not like that, you know; you fake it.
It's really rather dull.

# Intimates

Don't you care for my love? she said bitterly.

I handed her the mirror, and said:
Please address these questions to the proper person!
Please make all requests to head-quarters!
In all matters of emotional importance
please approach the supreme authority direct!
So I handed her the mirror.

And she would have broken it over my head,
but she caught sight of her own reflection
and that held her spellbound for two seconds
while I fled.

## Natural Complexion

But, you see, said the handsome young man with the chamois gloves
to the woman rather older than himself,
if you don't use rouge and a lip-stick, in Paris,
they'll take you for a woman of the people.

So spoke the British gentleman
pulling on his chamois gloves
and using his most melodious would-be-oxford voice.

And the woman said: Dear me!
how rough that would be on you, darling!
Only, if you insist on pulling on those chamois gloves
I swear I'll pull off my knickers, right in the Rue de la Paix.

## True Love at Last

The handsome and self-absorbed young man
looked at the lovely and self-absorbed girl
and thrilled.

The lovely and self-absorbed girl
looked back at the handsome and self-absorbed young man
and thrilled.

And in that thrill he felt:
Her self-absorption is even as strong as mine.
I must see if I can't break through it
and absorb her in me.

And in that thrill she felt:
His self-absorption is even stronger than mine!
What fun, stronger than mine!
I must see if I can't absorb this Samson of self-absorption.

So they simply adored one another
and in the end they were both nervous wrecks, because
In self-absorption and self-interest they were equally matched.

## The Painter's Wife

She was tangled up in her own self-conceit, a woman,
and her passion could only flare through the meshes
towards other women, in communion;
the presence of a man made her recoil
and burn blue and cold, like the flame in a miner's lamp
when the after-damp is around it.

Yet she seemed to know nothing about it
and devoted herself to her husband
and made him paint her nude, time after time,
and each time it came out the same, a horrible sexless, lifeless
    abstraction
of the female form, technically 'beautiful', actually a white machine
    drawing, more null than death.

And she was so pleased with it, she thought one day it would be
    recognised as 'great'.
And he thought so too.
Nobody else did.

# *[I Know a Noble Englishman]*

I know a noble Englishman
One of nature's gentlemen
Don't you know!
Eked out by his tailor and his hatter
And the Rock of Ages of his public school.

This noble gentleman
Is nothing if not normal
A great coureur de femmes.
Speaking of 'perverts', he takes on an amused, but icy contempt,
Himself so superior.

However
One of his beloveds, looking rather a wreck
After an affair with this noble Englishman
Said: Ronald, you see, is quite a clever sadist:
He's most frightfully skilful in his love-making
And makes a point of being very gentle, very tender
Don't you know?
And he *is* very gentle and tender—

Till he's got a woman a bit soft and trustful
Then he turns away and wipes her from his consciousness
As if she were a worm, or a hired whore who bored him,
An absolute nothing.

So the poor thing is left feeling an utter worm.
Not good enough to be loved by this expert.

But it's all a trick.
I've realised it is all a trick on his part.
He never wants a woman, he doesn't like women,
They are really repugnant to him.
So he cleverly plays the normal, the Don Juan
To make them feel absolute worms
Under his noble boot-sole.

As a matter of fact,
If the mean devil has any sex-feeling at all
It is for men: he's an instinctive homosexual,
Like almost all Englishmen.
But he's far too great a coward ever to admit his instincts.

Too great a boor to realise his true feelings.
Too great a skunk to abide by his own self
Too dirty a hypocrite to admit his own nature.
He shows an amused superior contempt at the prevalence of
    sodomy
And is himself normal, a lover of women.

But ask the women!
Ask all the women he's ever had
What about him.

The dirty little Don Juan
Balking his own nature
And taking it out on women
Leaving them crushed worms
And going blandly on to his next spite.

Every single erection of his is an erection of mean spite.

Don Juan! If you ask me
Don Juan was never anything but a self-thwarted sodomist
Taking it out, in spite, on women.

# THE DARK DOORS

The dying of desire, and the desire to die: poems from Lawrence's last year.

# Stop It

The one thing the old will never understand
is that you can't prevent change.
All flows, and even the old are rapidly flowing away.
And the young are flowing in the throes of a great
    alteration.

# Beautiful Old Age

It ought to be lovely to be old
to be full of the peace that comes of experience
and wrinkled ripe fulfilment.

The wrinkled smile of completeness that follows a life
lived undaunted and unsoured with accepted lies.
If people lived without accepting lies
they would ripen like apples, and be scented like pippins
in their old age.

Soothing, old people should be, like apples
when one is tired of love.
Fragrant like yellowing leaves, and dim with the soft
stillness and satisfaction of autumn.

And a girl should say:
It must be wonderful to live and grow old.
Look at my mother, how rich and still she is!

And a young man should think: By Jove
my father has faced all weathers, but it's been a life!

# Desire Goes Down into the Sea

I have no desire any more
towards woman or man, bird, beast or creature or thing.
All day long I feel the tide rocking, rocking

though it strikes no shore
in me.

Only mid-ocean—

# Desire is Dead

Desire may be dead
and still a man can be
a meeting place for sun and rain
wonder outwaiting pain
as in a wintry tree.

# Desire

Ah, in the past, towards rare individuals
I have felt the pull of desire:
Oh come, come nearer, come into touch!
Come physically nearer, be flesh to my flesh—

But say little, oh say little,
and afterwards, leave me alone.
Keep your aloneness, leave me my aloneness.
I used to say this, in the past, but now no more.
It has always been a failure.
They have always insisted on love
and on talking about it
and on the me-and-thee and what we meant to each
    other.

So now I have no desire any more
Except to be left, in the last resort, alone, quite alone.


# Gladness of Death

Oh death
about you I know nothing, nothing—
about the afterwards
as a matter of fact, we know nothing

Yet oh death, oh death
also I know so much about you
the knowledge is within me, without being a matter of fact.

And so I know
after the painful, painful experience of dying
there comes an after-gladness, a strange joy
in a great adventure
oh the great adventure of death, where Thomas Cook cannot guide
    us.

I have always wanted to be as the flowers are
so unhampered in their living and dying,
and in death I believe I shall be as the flowers are.
I shall blossom like a dark pansy, and be delighted
there among the dark sun-rays of death.
I can feel myself unfolding in the dark sunshine of death
to something flowery and fulfilled, and with a strange sweet
    perfume.
Men prevent one another from being men
but in the great spaces of death
the winds of the afterwards kiss us into blossom of manhood.

# *Bavarian Gentians*

Not every man has gentians in his house
In soft September, at slow, sad Michaelmas.

Bavarian gentians, tall and dark, but dark
Darkening the day-time torch-like with the smoking blueness of
    Pluto's gloom,
Ribbed hellish flowers erect, with their blaze of darkness spread blue
Blown flat into points, by the heavy white draught of the day.

Torch-flowers of the blue-smoking darkness, Pluto's dark-blue blaze
Black lamps from the halls of Dis, smoking dark blue
Giving off darkness, blue darkness, upon Demeter's yellow-pale day
whom have you come for, here in the white-cast day?

Reach me a gentian, give me a torch!
Let me guide myself with the blue, forked torch of a flower
Down the darker and darker stairs, where blue is darkened on
    blueness
Down the way Persephone goes, just now, in first-frosted
    September,
To the sightless realm where darkness is married to dark
And Persephone herself is but a voice, as a bride
A gloom invisible enfolded in the deeper dark
Of the arms of Pluto as he ravishes her once again
And pierces her once more with his passion of the utter dark.
Among the splendour of black-blue torches, shedding fathomless
    darkness on the nuptials.

Give me a flower on a tall stem, and three dark flames,
For I will go to the wedding, and be wedding-guest
At the marriage of the living dark.

# The Ship of Death

Have you built your ship of death, Oh have you?
Oh build your ship of death, for you will need it.

Now in the twilight, sit by the invisible sea
Of peace, and build your little ship
Of death, that will carry the soul
On its last journey, on and on, so still
So beautiful, over the last of seas.
When the day comes, that will come.
Oh think of it in the twilight peacefully!
The last day, and the setting forth
On the longest journey, over the hidden sea
To the last wonder of oblivion.

Oblivion, the last wonder!
When we have trusted ourselves entirely
To the unknown, and are taken up
Out of our little ships of death
Into pure oblivion.

Oh build your ship of death, be building it now
With dim, calm thoughts and quiet hands
Putting its timbers together in the dusk,
Rigging its mast with the silent, invisible sail
That will spread in death to the breeze
Of the kindness of the cosmos, that will waft
The little ship with its soul to the wonder-goal.

Ah, if you want to live in peace on the face of the earth
Then build your ship of death, in readiness
For the longest journey, over the last of seas.

# All Soul's Day

Be careful, then, and be gentle about death.
For it is hard to die, it is difficult to go through
the door, even when it opens.

And the poor dead, when they have left the walled
and silvery city of the now hopeless body
where are they to go, O where are they to go?

They linger in the shadow of the earth.
The earth's long conical shadow is full of souls
that cannot find the way across the sea of change.

Be kind, Oh be kind to your dead
and give them a little encouragement
and help them to build their little ship of death.

For the soul has a long, long journey after death
to the sweet home of pure oblivion.
Each needs a little ship, a little ship
and the proper store of meal for the longest journey.

Oh, from out of your heart
provide for your dead once more, equip them
like departing mariners, lovingly.

# NOTES

*General textual note*   The poem text is as printed in Lawrence's *Collected Poems* of 1928 unless otherwise indicated. The original publication is noted, using the following abbreviations: *A - Amores* 1916; *ALP - Last Poems* 1932; *BBF - Birds, Beasts and Flowers* 1923; *CP - Collected Poems* 1928; *LP - Love Poems and Others* 1913; *LWH - Look! We Have Come Through!* 1917; *NP - New Poems* 1918; *P - Pansies* June 1929 (unexpurgated edition). Other abbreviated titles: *Not I ...* - Frieda Lawrence; *Not I but the Wind; Phoenix - The Posthumous Papers of D. H. Lawrence; Phoenix II - Uncollected, Unpublished and Other Prose Works of D. H. Lawrence; Worthen* - John Worthen, *D. H. Lawrence: The Early Years; Chambers* - E. T. (Jessie Chambers), *D. H. Lawrence: A Personal Record; Carswell* - Catherine Carswell, *The Savage Pilgrimage; DHLR - The D. H. Lawrence Review. Complete Poems* refers to the Vivian de Sola Pinto and Warren Roberts text.

*General note on Lawrence's use of mythology*   One myth of seasonal fertility, of death and rebirth, was particularly important to Lawrence's poetry. Persephone (or Proserpina) was the daughter of Demeter (or Ceres), goddess and earth-mother. Her name originally connoted 'fruit-bearing'. Delighting in the meadows of Sicily, while gathering flowers in the fields of Enna, she was abducted by Pluto (otherwise 'Dis'), and carried into the underworld to be his bride (*cf* 'The Bride'). Her mother sought her, in her grief not allowing the earth to produce fruit or crops. When she discovered what had happened, Demeter demanded the return of her daughter, which was allowed on condition that Persephone had eaten nothing in the underworld; but Pluto had induced her to eat part of a pomegranate, so her return was limited to half of the year. As queen of the underworld, Persephone presided over the death of humankind – death itself required her or one of her Fates to cut off a hair, and Persephone was honoured by offerings of hair from the dead or the dying (*cf* 'Sorrow'). The Eleusinian mysteries at Athens were celebrated in honour of Persephone and Demeter. In Lawrence's poetry, Persephone is regularly associated with his mother, imagined as the compelled or captive bride to a husband associated with the underworld (the pit or death), with flowers ('Purple Anemones', 'Bavarian Gentians') or fruit ('Pomegranate') and with the landscape of Sicily. Earlier poems influencing Lawrence would include Meredith's 'The Appeasement of Demeter' and Swinburne's 'Hymn to Proserpine'.

# Early Love Poems

'Cherry Robbers'    Before January 1909. *LP*. See *Sons and Lovers*, chapter 11 (Penguin, p. 347–9). Hagg Farm had 'two fine cherry trees' (*Chambers*, p. 20).

'After School'    *c.* February 1909. Unpublished by Lawrence. Text, Nottingham University Library Ms La L 2.

'Wedding Morn'    *c.* 1911. *LP*. A typical matrimonial *aubade:* the song not of lovers who must part at dawn, but of lovers who are starting on life together. The moment when one character comes to full knowledge of the nature of another is also a characteristic motif.

'Love on the Farm'    Early 1907. *LP* with title 'Cruelty and Love'. Jessie Chambers pointed out that the poem is 'a sort of epitome' of the early version of *The White Peacock*: see the 'Poem of Friendship' chapter in the novel (*Chambers*, p. 116).

'Aware'    *LP*. Jessie Chambers annotates: 'It was at Christmas, 1909, that he made the great effort to resolve the conflict in himself. Soon after my return from London he sent me the verse "Aware", but I had always been careful not to take his poems too literally' (*Chambers*, p. 180).

'Lightning'        First drafts from *c.* 1906–8. *The Nation*, 4 November 1911. Lawrence had an early version of this poem put into his first volume, *LP*, despite its non-selection by his editor, Walter de la Mare.

'Lilies in the Fire'        May 1910. *LP*. Third poem from a sequence dealing with the failed love-making with 'Miriam'.

'Sigh No More'        Summer 1910. *The English Review*, October 1910, and *NP*. Title from *Much Ado About Nothing* II iii. See Introduction for comment.

'Seven Seals'        *NP*. The Seven Seals derive from *Revelations*, chapters 5–7. The archaic vocabulary ('Champaign' – field, 'Chrism' – holy oil, 'mort' – a horn blown at a death) and figurative language are unusual: perhaps fantasy is closer than autobiography.

'Last Words to Miriam'        December 1910. *A*. The third stanza is Lawrence's major addition to a much revised poem.

'Yew-Tree on the Downs'        Summer–autumn 1910. *A* with title 'Liaison'. The poem can be associated with Helen Corke, with whom Lawrence went for walks in Kent. They were probably never lovers (*Worthen*, p. 258).

'Kisses in the Train'        1911. *LP*. The woman in the poem is Lawrence's fiancée, Louie Burrows. Lawrence proposed to her in a train (*Worthen*, p. 291). In the final stanza, the text in *LP* read 'Her own to my perfect' for 'My own to her perfect'. A magnet's 'keeper' is a metal bar joining the two poles of a horseshoe magnet, preventing the loss of magnetic flux.

'Snap-Dragon'        1911. *The English Review*, June 1912, and *A*. About Louie Burrows, apparently written when she challenged him to produce a love poem (*Worthen*, p. 552). See *Letters* I, p. 403 (after sending a copy to Frieda): 'I would never write like that to you.' 'Reiver bird' – a robber bird, here, the cuckoo. Jessie Chambers recollected Lawrence giving her the poem 'with a significant glance' (*Chambers*, p. 142): her love presumably being the fledgling ousted from the nest.

'Turned Down'        Date between 1911 and publication in *The Egoist*, 1 April 1914 (as 'Fooled'), then *A*. Also in *Some Imagist Poets* (1916). The scene setting could relate it to the 'relationship in London with a woman he called "Jane" of whom we know nothing' (*Worthen*, p. 251).

'Sickness'        *NP*. Lawrence suffered double pneumonia, November- –December 1911. Louie Burrows was not allowed to visit him.

'Pear-Blossom'        *c*. April 1912. Unpublished by Lawrence, from a notebook in the Library of the University of Nottingham. Possibly about Lawrence's affair with Alice Dax, or one of his first poems about Frieda (*Worthen*, pp. 383, 566), though 'small breasts' does not fit his other descriptions of the latter; 'poppy-show' is a dialect version of 'puppet-show' or a 'peep-show'.

'Forecast'        *c*. 1910? *A* with title 'Epilogue'. The verse epistle is from a woman predicting her lover's fate if he leaves her. See Holly Laird, *Self and Sequence*, p. 63.

# Narratives

The main features of the North Midlands dialect Lawrence reproduces in the following poems are broader vowel sounds, the syncopation of the definite article, and the substitution of 'thee' and 'tha' for 'you', 'sen' for 'self'. See *Worthen*, pp. 62–4, for Lawrence's brilliant mimicry of dialect.

'Violets'        *c*. January 1909. *The Nation*, 4 November 1911, and *LP*. In the first version of this poem, 'Violets for the Dead', there is no rain during the burial. Lawrence's mother was buried in pouring rain on 12 December 1910, after which Lawrence wore violets from a wreath on his journey back to Croydon (*Worthen*, p. 287). 'An' a' t' black' – and all the black, i.e. mourning garments; 't' pad' – the path; 'what 'er 'ad on' – what she intended to do; 'slive' – creep; 'scraightin' – weeping; 'maun' – must.

'Whether or Not'      *c.* August–November 1911, last section 1927. *LP*, text *CP*. Revision, beside verbal changes and heightening of the dialect, included the addition of the final section: 'How well I remember the evenings at [Edward] Garnett's house in Kent, by the log fire. And there I wrote the best of the dialect poems. I remember Garnett disliked the old ending to "Whether or Not". Now I see he was right, it was the voice of the commonplace me, not the demon. So I have altered it.' (From Foreword to *CP*.) Part II: 'sludged' – slogged, toiled laboriously; 'whit-leather' – cured horse hide, used for protective gloves, etc; 'slive' – creep; 'otchel' – humpback(?); Part III: 'Brinsley', 'Underwood' – the poem can be read exactly on to the map of 'The Lawrence Country' in F. B. Pinion's *A D. H. Lawrence Companion* (Macmillan, 1978, p. 9). Part IV; 'pee-whips' – peewits (the lapwing); 'smock-ravelled' – perplexed; 'larropin' – trailing through; Part V: see Pinion's map for the level-crossing. Part VI: 'Yi, tha must ha' bin 'ard ter wean' – still a baby, readily credulous (i.e. when he believes her story that the widow is getting married); 'ter ha'e me on' – deceive me; 'clawkin' – greedy, consuming; 'I h 'arena' – I'm not; ' "'E up an' fired 'is pistol,/An' then away 'e ran!" ' – quotation untraced, a comic poem mocking a cowardly male is indicated; Part VII: 'colleyfoglin' – wheedling, scheming; 'orts and slarts' – leavings and droppings; Part VIII: ' 'affle an' caffle' – haggle; 'cabs an' rice' – adjuncts of a church wedding.

'The Drained Cup'      1913. *LP*. 'Frit' – frightened; 'flig' – eager (of birds: ready for flight).

'The Young Soldier with Bloody Spurs'      Unpublished by Lawrence, text from *Letters*. Sent by Lawrence to Edward Garnett, 13 August 1912: 'It is rather long, but good, I think.' See *Mr Noon*, chapter 19, for the same incident, and Gilbert's reaction: 'his heart burned to be with the men' (pp. 263–6).

# The Virgin Mother

Lawrence's love for his mother is the theme of this section. It is an essential and unparalleled aspect of his output as a love poet. Though the subject matter is unusual, it is in these poems that Lawrence most closely approximates to the conventions of desperate yearning, adulation and self-dedication which have typified the poetry of frustrated love (see Introduction). Yet the poems also capture the struggle to break free recorded in *Sons and Lovers*.

'Discord in Childhood'     *c.* November 1909. *A.* The foreword to *CP* records Lawrence's belief that he had destroyed the long poem of which this was a 'fragment', but see the fuller text of 'A Life History in Harmonies and Discords' retrieved by *Worthen* (pp. 274–6 and his Appendix III). Version of the same recollection in *Sons and Lovers*, chapter 4 (Penguin, p. 78).

'Monologue of a Mother'     Winter 1909–10. Early versions in *Poetry*, January 1914, (as 'A Mother of Sons') and *A.* Lawrence was the third son of Arthur John Lawrence and Lydia Beardsall, after George Arthur and William Earnest. A 'weird' is a prediction (archaic/poetic).

'End of Another Home Holiday'     *c.* August 1909. *LP.* The family had in fact spent the first two weeks of August on the Isle of Wight. Mrs Lawrence's illness first became apparent during the holiday.

'The Bride'     1910–11. *A.* The version published in *Young Lorenzo* (1932) is entitled 'The Dead Mother'. Lydia Lawrence died 9 December 1910. See *Sons and Lovers*, Chapter 14 (Penguin, p. 485).

'The Virgin Mother'     December 1910. *A.* Frieda annotated a four-stanza first version, 'My Love, My Mother', with 'I hate it' opposite stanzas 1, 2, 4 (here 1, 2, 3), 'You love it, you say!!!!' after stanza 1, and 'Good God' and '!!!!!' against the cancelled third stanza, which ran:

*You sweet love, my mother*
*Twice you have blooded me,*
*Once with your blood at birth time*
*Once with your misery.*
*And twice you have washed me clean,*
*Twice-wonderful things to me.*

See her further response in *Worthen*, p. 412, and notes on 'Everlasting Flowers for a Dead Mother'.

'Sorrow'      December 1910. Published *Poetry*, December 1914, (with the title 'Weariness') and *A*, despite Lawrence's comment on the poem being one of 'two bits of verse I don't want publishing' (*Letters* I, p. 254). See *Sons and Lovers* (Penguin, p. 457).

'Listening'      December 1910. *A*.

'Piano'      First drafts from *c.* 1906–8 (see Holly Laird, *DHLR* 1985–6, for a discussion of the poem's evolution and critical impact). *NP*. See *The White Peacock* Part 1 chapter I (Cambridge, p. 6–7). Lawrence would have known Verlaine's 'Le piano que baise une main frele' in *Romances sans Paroles*. See *Worthen* (pp. 34, 39) for the purchase of the second-hand 'Pianette' and its importance as a status-symbol in 'Piano Row' (i.e. Walker Street) and Lawrence's defence: 'The middle classes jeer at the colliers for buying pianos – but what is the piano, often as not, but a blind reaching out for beauty?' ('Nottingham and the Mining Countryside' *Phoenix*, p. 138). For one subsequent instrument, read Frieda's description of a piano's delivery by small boat to the cottage at Spezia (*Not I . . .*, Heinemann, 1935, p. 66). 'Appassionato' is the musical direction for impassioned performance; the poem's title and first word involve a subdued pun, piano = softly.

# *From* Look! We Have Come Through!

*Look! We Have Come Through!* was published in December 1917. Most of the poems were written in the year from May 1912 to April 1913, with a concentration in the summer months of 1912. Lawrence rewrote the poems for publication in January and February 1917, with the projected title 'Man and Woman'. *Carswell* (p. 89) testifies that Lawrence said the sequence '"might as well . . . have been called *And Now Farewell*," as it marked "a sort of conclusion of the old life" in him.' Re-arranging *Look!* for the 1928 *Collected Poems*, he brought 'Bei Hennef' and 'Everlasting Flowers' into the sequence. *Look!* has a chronological sequence, preserved in this selection.

It is important to realise that when Frieda Weekley went to Germany with Lawrence (3 May 1912) there was every chance that she would return to her husband and children. She had previously taken a lover while on one of her long summer visits to her family. Lawrence saw what they had done as elopement for the purpose of marriage, when legally possible ('I know in my heart "here's my marriage"' (*Letters* I, p. 403), but Frieda had vowed never to marry again (*ibid*, p. 409) and was only slowly persuaded (e.g. *Letters* I, p. 489: 'Frieda says she's not keen on marrying me – but I want some peace'). The sequence of poems deals with their mutuality and mutual dissatisfaction within this difficult situation, and leads to the triumphant self-epithalamion of 'Song of a Man Who Has Come Through', written around the date of his marriage to Frieda, 13 July 1914.

Many of the poems find inspiration in the beautiful countryside the lovers stayed in and walked through on their journey from Icking on the River Isar in Germany, through Austria towards Italy. Lawrence and Frieda finally settled at the Villa Igea near Gargano on the Lago di Garda.

'Hymn to Priapus'    Written early 1912(?). *The English Review*, September 1917, with the title 'Constancy of a Sort'. The poem probably antedates Lawrence meeting Frieda for the first time (March 1912), and should not be used to suggest that the subject of *Look!* is physical marriage to Frieda succeeding spiritual marriage to his mother. Extensive discussion in Murfin, *The Poetry of D. H. Lawrence*.

'Ballad of a Wilful Woman'    Written 9–11 May 1912 while Lawrence waited for Frieda in Trier, inventing a myth for her: the woman leaves her husband for the life of the flesh (Cytherea is the island of love), and then for the spirit (St John the Divine lived on the island of Patmos), before taking up with the beggar, Lawrence, who despite his poverty offers a synthesis of flesh and spirit. See *Letters* II, pp. 94, 104, for Lawrence's varied thoughts on the ballad's merit. *Worthen* gives details of how accurate the prediction of impoverished wanderings turned out to be. The 'flame-wild drops' of Part VI clearly symbolise Lawrence's writings, but Frieda notes his fondness for making an infusion out of gathered rue.

'Bei Hennef'    11 May. *LP*, brought into the *Look!* sequence for *CP*. Sandra Gilbert suggests that writing this poem was a 'turning point morally and artistically' for Lawrence, and that his memories of the compositional experience 'may have helped determine the poetics he was to outline in "Poetry of the Present", of verse "instantaneous like plasm"' (Gilbert, *Acts of Attention*, 1990, pp. 88–9).

'First Morning'    26 May. *Mr Noon* (p. 204) repeats the setting, and gives both sides to the dialogue: ' "The night was a failure," he said. "It was, wasn't it?" "Well, why not?" "Ha – I suppose one can't always be happy," she sighed.' Note that Lawrence and Frieda seem to have been lovers in England, before going abroad. 'Pappus' is the botanical term for the down which helps a dandelion seed fly.

'Frohnleichnam'    6 June. The title means 'joyful body', Corpus Christi day is Frohnleichnamstag. The poem, celebrating a 'heaven of our own' against a background of preparations for the feast in Wolfratshausen, develops the *Look!* sequence's mixing of religion and love. For the publisher's objections to this aspect, see *Letters* III, p. 145. 'World without end' – from *The Book of Common Prayer*, Morning Prayer, Gloria; 'throw immortality off' – the orthodox Christian desire would be to 'throw off' mortality, the body.

'A Young Wife'    Lines 7–8 *cf* 'In the Dark' (*Complete Poems* p. 210–2): 'My dear, when you cross the street in the sunshine, surely/

Your own small night goes with you. Why treat it so poorly?' Allan
Ingram (*The Language of D. H. Lawrence*, Macmillan 1990, p. 24)
notes the hymn-book rhythms of this poem.

'Green'          Lawrence's later copying out of this poem as a postscript to
a letter (31 March 1920) argues his pleasure in it. Verlaine, one of the
'two great poetic lights in his firmament' (with Baudelaire – *Chambers*,
p. 121), has a poem of the same title in *Aquarelles*.

'Gloire de Dijon'          First printed with the following poem in *Poetry*,
January 1914, as parts of a short sequence, 'All of Roses', quoted
complete by Frieda in *Not I . . . .* 'Gloire de Dijon' is Lawrence's one
entry in Betjeman and Taylor's *English Love Poems*.

'Roses on the Breakfast Table'/'I am Like a Rose'/'Rose of all the
World'          For the dialogue with Yeats implied in the titles of these
rose poems, see Introduction. See the essay 'Love' (*Phoenix*, p. 153-5)
for the rose as a symbol of the union of sacred and profane love in the
conjunction of man and woman; *Letters* I, p. 402 (15 May 1912) for
Frieda's possible pregnancy; *Letters* II, p. 103, for Lawrence's scansion
of the first poem. 'Orts and slarts' – leavings and droppings (see
'Whether or Not'); 'urgent will in me, to set/My mouth on hers in
kisses' – not always the case in Lawrence's erotics, see Mellors in *Lady
Chatterley's Lover* (Penguin, p. 131) 'He hated mouth kisses'; 'bush/
Which burnt' – see *Exodus* 3:2, God speaks to Moses from a burning
bush, to announce the delivery of Israel from Egypt.

'Quite Forsaken'          Throughout the sequence, exploitation of the
symbolic potential of the weather, the landscape or its human activities
is recurrent. See *Mr Noon* (chapter 19, p. 292) for a reworking of the
same incident.

'A Doe at Evening'          Written in 1913 at Irschenhausen, and inserted
into the *Look!* sequence among the poems of 1912. The imaginative
self-metamorphosis looks forwawrd to 'Mountain Lion'; 'cover' suggests 'conceal, hide from view', but also 'overlap with, cover the same
area as'. See *Mr Noon* (chapter 19, pp. 271-2) for the sighting.

'Sinners'     Written in the happy week spent at Mayrhofen (from 10
August 1912) while waiting for David Garnett and Harold Hobson. *Mr
Noon* (p. 320) gives the picnic lunches and the 'ravings' in letters from
Ernest Weekley ('A fallen woman, a pariah in society', etc.).

'Everlasting Flowers for a Dead Mother'     Written possibly
November 1912, published *NP*. Lawrence may have brought this
spooky poem into the 1928 arrangement of *Look!* with some memory
of the quarrel over 'The Virgin Mother' which occurred at about this
point in the events covered by the *Look!* sequence. See notes to that
poem. 'Everlasting Flowers' – helichrysum, used in dry flower
arrangements; 'my little darling' *cf* the opening of 'The Virgin Mother'.
For two omitted stanzas, see *Letters* III, p. 283.

'Sunday Afternoon in Italy'     *c.* October 1912. For the contest of
bride and groom, backed by villagers of their sex, see *Women in Love*
(Cambridge, pp. 18–9; pp. 515–6 give the fine first version, which
Lawrence nevertheless succeeded in improving).

'All Souls'     All Souls' Day is 2 November. On the eve, candles are
lit in cemeteries to commemorate the dead, and on the day prayers are
said for the departed who are still in purgatory, though Lawrence's
'other world' (1.22) is evidently Heaven. Catholic ceremonies wit-
nessed by Lawrence and Frieda at Gargano, for the candle figure, see
*Letters* I, p. 503.

'Both Sides of the Medal'     December 1912. Harold Hobson was
spending Christmas at the Villa Igea. Lawrence had already forgiven
Frieda for making love with him. See *Worthen*, p. 428–30, and *Letters* I,
p. 488, for Hobson as Frieda's 'friend'. 'Balaam's ass', seeing the angel of
the Lord about to kill Balaam on his way to assist the Moabites against
Israel, hinders his journey, and when beaten, speaks to him before
Balaam himself sees the angel *Numbers* 22:22–34. For the 'balanced,
eternal orbit', see *Women in Love*, p. 319.

'Loggerheads'     The first stanza refers to testing whether gold or
silver coinage is real or forged by making the metal ring, and stanza two

to sugar adulterated with sand by unscrupulous grocers. A 'weeping willow' is the traditional haunt of the disappointed lover.

'December Night'        'My hearth . . . I have made the fire up bright' – Lawrence took pride in housework. See *Worthen*, p. 49–50, and Major Eastwood in *The Virgin and the Gypsy*.

'Paradise Re-entered'        Early 1913. The formally intricate rhyme scheme this poem gradually adopts is evidently chosen to convey a ceremonial climax. Lawrence was 'suspicious' of this poem, but 'inclined to think' that it was good (*Letters* II, p. 104). He did revise for *CP* 'our awful embraces', to 'awed'. Vocabulary in stanza two recalls *The Rainbow* (Cambridge, p. 443): '[Skrebensky] felt himself fusing down to nothingness, like a bead that rapidly disappears in an incandescent flame', and a more general resemblance to the figure of passing through a doorway, used to describe the renewal of passion after alienation, *The Rainbow* (end of chapter 3).

'History'        A retrospective poem of July 1913.

'Song of a Man Who has Come Through'        Written around the date of Lawrence's marriage to Frieda, 13 July 1914. Keith Sagar has suggested that the wind in this poem recalls the wind which accompanies Tom Brangwen when he goes to ask Lydia to marry him (*The Rainbow*, chapter 1). Lawrence finished the first version of the novel in May 1914. 'Hesperides' – in myth, the paradisal garden where Jason sought the Golden Fleece. In 'We have gone too far' (*Complete Poems*, p. 737) Lawrence refers to 'The lost Hesperides where love is pure'. The 'three strange angels' probably refer to *Genesis* xviii. They arrive to foretell the birth of a son to Abraham and Sarah; Lawrence refers to them in *The Rainbow* chapter 11 (Cambridge, p. 271).

# The Work of Creation

(For the poem which provided the title of this section, see *Complete Poems*.)

'Michael-Angelo'     *c.* 1911. I have chosen the version from *LP* over the revision for *CP*, which loses the startling ending (for which Lawrence cut five further stanzas from his first draft) and is vitiated by self-conscious reminiscences of Blake's 'The Tyger'. See *Sons and Lovers* (Penguin, p. 239).

'Pomegranate' and 'Peach'     September 1920. *BBF*. Two poems in which Lawrence insists on seeing a gendered femininity in the fruit, to the annoyance of his addressee (*cf Letters* I, p. 657: '"Pomegranate" in the singular, I think'). See also 'Andraitx' in *Complete Poems*. Syracuse is a 'rock left bare by the viciousness of Greek women' because, in Frieda's words (about the Peloponnesian war): 'Here at Syracuse the flower of the Athenian youth had been defeated; in these quarries the Greek men had been put to starve while the ladies of Syracuse took their walks along the top of the quarries to see them slowly die. A sinister dread impression it left in me. I doubt whether centuries can clean a place of such inhumanity, the place will retain and remember such horrors' (*Not I . . .*, p. 105).

'Purple Anemones'     *BBF*. Written 4 February 1921 and sent to his American literary agent, Robert Mountsier, as 'a nice flower poem' on the 5th, Lawrence not keeping a copy. For the flowers, see *Letters* III, p. 683, or the essay 'Flowery Tuscany', which re-uses the baying hounds figure (*Phoenix*, pp. 50, 52). See general note on Lawrence's mythology.

'Snake'     July 1920. *The Dial*, July 1921, and *BBF*. Sent to Robert Mountsier 25 January 1921, Lawrence not keeping a copy. For the setting, see *Letters* III, p. 489: 'The ancient fountain still runs, in a sort of cave-place down the garden – the Fontana Vecchia – and still supplies us.' Frieda's casual recollection of 'getting water from the trough near the wall, where the large yellow snake came to drink and drew itself into its hole in the wall again' (*Not I . . .*, p. 106) suggests that Lawrence made dramatic a recurrent visitation. The voices of Lawrence's education were ill-informed. The 'earth-brown, earth-golden' snake, described by Frieda as 'large', was probably the Montpellier snake, *Coelopeltis monspessulana*. It can be six feet long, but has only mild venom in teeth set too far back to harm anything larger than rodents. The black snakes are the European whip snake, *Zamenis gemonensis*, common in Italy. Black specimens occur in some island locations in its range. The only dangerous European snakes are vipers, with bold dark markings and they are relatively small.

Lawrence had written many poems finding a sexual symbolism in flora and fauna: was he unaware of his readily decipherable subject here, sodomy, especially after his use of the 'serpent of abhorrence' symbol in *The Reality of Peace* (*Phoenix*, p. 678): 'I must own my most secret shame and my most secret shameful desire'.? 'Albatross' – in Coleridge's 'Rime of the Ancient Mariner', the mariner is cursed for shooting the albatross.

'Tortoise Family Connections' and 'Tortoise Shout'      September 1920, and first published in *Tortoises*, 1921, then *BBF*. *Letters* III, pp. 607–9, expresses Lawrence's pleasure in his sequence of tortoise poems, from which I have chosen a poem wryly reflecting on an early life without the maternal tie, and one about sex. Lawrence's sisters 'loftily disapproved' of the *Tortoises* sequence (*Carswell*, p. 168). See 'On Being a Man' (*Phoenix* II, p. 619) for further reflections from Lawrence on marriage as 'the inevitable crucifixion'. 'Woman, what have I to do with thee' – *John* 2:4 (authorized version); 'Basta!' – that's enough!

'The Ass'      *BBF*. Written 2 March 1921, then misplaced (*Letters* IV, p. 201) and re-discovered (IV, p. 319). In *Sea and Sardinia* (chapter I) Lawrence re-uses the Arab interpretation of the ass's bray. *'Noli me tangere'* – *John* 20:17, Vulgate version ('Touch me not').

'She-Goat'      *BBF*. December–January 1922. De Sola Pinto and Roberts give translations for the Italian phrases (they are in Sicilian dialect): *'Tace, tu, crapa, bestia!'* – Shut up, you, she-goat, animal!; *'Le bestie non parlano, poverine!'* – The animals do not talk, poor things.

'Fish'     *BBF*. August 1921, a poem described by Lawrence as one of only two things he wrote during that summer. In this poem Lawrence considers an existence and sexuality which lies beyond his power of empathy. The Anapo is a Sicilian river, the Zeller lake is in the Austrian Alps.

'Mountain Lion'     *BBF*. Written January 1923 at the Del Monte Ranch. Frieda describes horseback expeditions into the Lobo canyon (*Not I . . .*, p. 129); more on the landscape in the essay 'New Mexico'. See Introduction for discussion. *'Qué tiene, amigo?'* – What are you carrying, friend? Note that *león* = lion, *leóna* is lioness; *'Hermoso es'* – He is beautiful.

'The Elephant is Slow to Mate'     *P*. Printed without spaces between the stanzas in the unexpurgated text of *P*.

'[Flat-foot's Song]'     July 1925. De Sola Pinto and Roberts' marvellous retrieval from 'Him with his Tail in his Mouth', *Reflections on the Death of a Porcupine* (1925), p. 136. 'His poem' because 'If I myself had to make a poem to her, I should begin:

> *Oh my flat-footed plush armchair*
> *So commonly scratching in the yard—!*

But this poem would only reveal my own limitations' (*ibid*, p. 135).

'Whales Weep Not!'     *ALP*. Lawrence quotes extensively from *Moby Dick*, Volume III 'The Grand Armada', in his essay on the novel, which provided him with the male defensive ring around suckling young and 'Leviathan amours in the deep'. Some readers will recollect that the poem is quoted by Captain Kirk in *Star Trek IV*.

# Lyrics, Proffered Wisdoms and Satires

## Lyrics

'Gipsy'     *NP*, last two stanzas from *Letters* VI, p. 389. These Lawrence claims he 'left out for [sic] the printed version'. See *Letters* I,
p. 196 (6 December 1910), for the original version, 'Self-Contempt',
sub-titled 'A laborer speaks' (sent to Louie Burrows three days after an
engagement which involved Lawrence confessing that he only had
£4 4s 2½d) and for his source. The poem evolved from male self-
abasement towards an erotic demand.

['Unfortunate Interrupted Lovers']     This quatrain is taken from
*Mr Noon*, chapter 16 (Cambridge, p. 152). The editorial title appears
in the text immediately after the verse.

'Leda'     *P*. Lawrence did a painting of this subject, 19–22 December
1928. See also 'The Crown' (*Phoenix* II, p. 403).

'Little Fish'/'Spray'/'Sea-weed'     *P*. 'They Say the Sea is Loveless'
*LP*. 'You' *P*. Lawrence gave a psycho-sexual significance to sea-weed in
*The Fox* (*The Short Novels*, Phoenix edition I, p. 66).

[*Three Poems in Wartime*]     Though he published *Bay* as a book of
war-related poems, Lawrence is not noted as a poet of World War One:
only one poem ('Song of a Man Who Has Come Through') gets into
Jon Silkin's *Penguin Book of First World War Poetry*. Critical studies by
Cushman and Laird have given most attention to the war-related
poems. The following three lyrics come from his 'tiny book of poems',
*Bits* (or 'All of Us'), which was never published. His letters of 11
December 1916 show his excitement with the series as potentially
successful 'war *literature*'.

'Maiden's Prayer'     In the projected *Bits*, the poem had a
descriptive title, 'Straying Thoughts: A girl goes to the cathedral
church, to pray for her beloved' (Holly Laird, *Self and Sequence*, p. 107).
'The Maiden's Prayer' was a very familiar piano piece, see 'Nottingham
and the Mining Countryside' *Phoenix*, p. 138.

'Swing Song' of a Girl and a Soldier     In *Bits* with sub-title 'A girl in a swing, and a soldier swinging her'. See *Sons and Lovers* (Penguin, p. 186–8) and Ursula and Skrebensky in *The Rainbow*, p. 274.

'The Jewess and the V.C.'        *Poetry*, July 1919, as part of the sequence from *Bits* entitled 'War Films'. In *Bits* as 'Elixir: A woman of the East encourages her young man, who is home on leave.' Laird (*Self and Sequence*, p. 107) says the poem began as a 'whimsical love lyric' for Louie Burrows. For the confrontation of Jewess and soldier, see *The Virgin and the Gypsy*. 'V.C.' – the Victoria Cross, the highest award for bravery in the British armed forces.

## Proffered Wisdoms

'Rainbow'        December 1926 (the month Lawrence began the second *Lady Chatterley*). Submitted to Edgell Rickword's *Calendar of Modern Letters* on New Year's Eve 1926, and published in Volume IV (April 1927), pp. 20–1.

'We are Transmitters'        *P.* The unexpurgated text reads 'ripping' for 'rippling'. 'Give, and it shall be given unto you': *Luke* 6:38.

'Sex Isn't Sin'        *P.* Lines 7–9 ('especially . . . is worse') omitted in the unexpurgated *P.*

'In a Spanish Tram-car'        *c.* May–June 1929. *ALP.* Lawrence was in Barcelona in April 1929.

'The Mess of Love'/'The Effort of Love'/'Chastity'        *P.*

'Lies about Love'        July 1929. *ALP.*

'Retort to Jesus'/'Commandments'        *ALP. cf* Blake 'The Everlasting Gospel', available to Lawrence in various late nineteenth- and early twentieth-century editions ('Was Jesus humble?' ll. 25–6):

> *He who loves his enemies betrays his friends*
> *This surely is not what Jesus intends.*

'Love our neighbour' – *Matthew* 22:39.

'Glimpses'/'For a Moment'        *ALP*. 'The broad and thick-set Italian':
Giuseppe Orioli, publisher of *Lady Chatterley* and *Last Poems*. The
woman is evidently Frieda. For the conceit of the poem, see *Mr Noon*,
chapter 4, where Gilbert observes Patty Goddard mutate into Aphrodite. 'It' (1.7) omitted in *ALP*, restored from ms.

'The Man of Tyre'        *ALP*. Elizabeth Cipolla (*DHLR*, 1969) suggests
Maximus of Tyre, a Greek Sophist who lived AD 125–85 inspired
Lawrence's man caught between doctrines. Line 2 parodies a line from
'I'll Sing You One-O/Green grow the rushes-O'.

'To Women, as Far as I'm Concerned'        *P*.

*Satires*
'All-knowing'        *ALP*.

'When I Went to the Film'/'Film Passion'        *P*. The dialogues of Mr
May and Alvina Houghton in chapter 6 of *The Lost Girl* give more of
Lawrence on the 'dithering eye-ache' of film. Rudolf Valentino, star of
*The Sheik* (1922) died of peritonitis on 23 August 1926. Lawrence
discusses his looks in 'Sex versus Loveliness' and prefers those of
Charlie Chaplin.

'No! Mr Lawrence'        *P*.

'Intimates'        *ALP*.

'Natural Complexion'        *P*.

'True Love at Last'        *ALP*. Line 3 omitted in the 1932 edition.

'The Painter's Wife'        June 1929. *ALP*. The discussion of Cezanne's
struggle to paint his wife in Lawrence's 'Introduction to his Paintings'
(1929) parallels the poem.

'[I Know a Noble Englishman]'        Unpublished version of 'The

Noble Englishman' in *P*, text from ms in the Library of the University of Texas.

# The Dark Doors

(For the poem which provided the title of this section, see 'Doors' in *Complete Poems*.)

'Stop It'    *P*.

'Beautiful Old Age'    *P*. 'Like apples/when one is tired of love' – *The Song of Solomon* 2:5 'comfort me with apples, for I am sick of love'.

'Desire Goes Down into the Sea'/'Desire is Dead'    *P*. Graham Hough notes the 'late-Yeatsian gnomic compactness' (*The Dark Sun*, p. 210) of the latter.

'Desire'/'Gladness of Death'    *ALP*.

'Bavarian Gentians'    September 1929 at Rottach. The text given here (from the appendix to *ALP*, line 10 restored from Lawrence's ms) follows the arguments of Keith Sagar (*DHLR* 1975). *Mr Noon* (chapter 13, p. 136) has Lawrence's record of 'for the first time in his life' seeing gentians 'so blue, again his heart seemed to break one of its limits, and take a larger swing'. Frieda (*Not I . . .*, pp. 33, 187) recalled both Lawrence's first gentian ('When Lawrence first found a gentian, a big single blue one, I remember feeling as if he had a strange communion with it') and his last, the 'enormous bunch of gentians I had put on the floor by his bed'. See the general note on Lawrence's mythology.

'The Ship of Death'    September 1929. Text from the appendix to *ALP*, following the arguments of Keith Sagar (*DHLR* 1987). Lawrence, who wrote his own epithalamion, also produced self-elegy. Christopher Hassall pointed out (in *A D. H. Lawrence Miscellany*, ed.

Harry T. Moore, Southern Illinois University Press, 1959) that the core image was developed from 'the little bronze ship of death' amongst artefacts in the tomb of the Etruscan Lucumo (seer/chief).

'All Soul's Day'      *ALP*. Probably written 2 November 1929. In this poem Lawrence re-visits impersonally the day of commemoration and fervent dedication to his mother of 'All Souls'.

Lawrence died 10 p.m., 2 March, 1930.

# FURTHER READING

'Most tedious was the close study of English Literature. Why should one remember the books one read?' Ursula's opinion about her school syllabus (*The Rainbow*, Chapter 12) serves to remind us that Lawrence would not have relished the academic study of his writings, unmediated engagement with a text being the requirement he made of all readers.

Lawrence expounded his own views about poetry in his 'Poetry of the Present', written as the preface to the American edition of *New Poems* in 1918 (he thought of calling the piece 'Verse Free and Unfree'). This preface drew upon Lawrence the most famous attack on his poetic – R. P. Blackmur's 'D. H. Lawrence and Expressive Form' in *Language as Gesture* (1954).

The chapters on Whitman in *Studies in Classic American Literature* and the introduction ('Chaos in Poetry') to Harry Crosby's *Chariot of the Sun* are the other important statements from Lawrence.

The prime source of understanding of this highly autobiographical poet comes from his life: the three-volume, multi-author Cambridge biography of D. H. Lawrence will be standard. The *Letters* in the Cambridge edition include indexes in each volume, with entries for the various books of poems and for individual poems. The Cambridge *Edition of the Letters and Works of D. H. Lawrence* will include a Variorum text of the poetry, edited by Carole Ferrier and Christopher Pollnitz. There is a concordance to the poetry, assembled by Reloy Gracia and James Karabatsos (Nebraska UP, 1971).

For those who feel impelled to know what others think, there are several full-length academic studies:

Sandra M. Gilbert, *Acts of Attention* (Cornell UP, 1972). The second edition, 1990, has an especially interesting preface where this noted feminist accounts for her interest in Lawrence. It remains the major critical study.

Holly A. Laird, *Self and Sequence* (University Press of Virginia, 1988) is a specialised study with some interesting things to say about the arrangement of the poems in Lawrence's *Collected Poems*, but goes too far: one poem, printed in what she considers an 'odd position', finally suggests to her that, 'Lawrence did not worry over every ligature of these poems.'

M. J. Lockwood, *A Study of the Poems of D. H. Lawrence* (Macmillan, 1987). A study with no settled purpose, but at least unafraid to pass critical judgement. Includes a full bibliography.

Gail Mandell, *The Phoenix Paradox: A Study of Renewal Through Change in the Collected Poems and Last Poems of D. H. Lawrence* (Southern Illinois UP, 1984). Largely concerned with Lawrence's use of myth. Fights shy of passing critical judgements.

Tom Marshall, *The Psychic Mariner* (Heinemann, 1970). An unspecialised, general account, which looks at a wide range of the poems.

Ross C. Murfin, *The Poetry of D. H. Lawrence: Texts and Contexts* (Nebraska UP, 1983). On the relation of Lawrence's poetry to antecedent texts. A narrow choice of poetic progenitors spoils the study (nothing on Lawrence and Verlaine, Lawrence and Meredith). Epitomised by the attempt to suggest that the 'three strange angels' of 'Song of a Man Who Has Come Through' can be seen as Whitman, Shelley and Tennyson.

Useful collections of material include:

R. P. Draper's *D. H. Lawrence: The Critical Heritage* (RKP, 1970), which includes contemporary reviews of Lawrence's verse. Stephen Spender's *D. H. Lawrence: Novelist, Poet, Prophet* (1973) has an essay by A. Alvarez, 'Lawrence's Poetry: The Single State of Man', and a notably enthusiastic account of *Look! We Have Come Through!* in Barbara Hardy's 'Women in D. H. Lawrence's Works'. A. Banerjee has edited *D. H. Lawrence's Poetry: Demon Liberated* (Macmillan, 1990), extracts from Lawrence on poetry and from critical assessments of variable value. The most Lawrentian is the extract from Kenneth Rexroth's *World Outside the Window* (written in 1947). Banerjee's compilation should be supplemented with Graham Hough's quotable overall view in his study, *The Dark Sun* (Duckworth, 1956), and Keith Sagar's discussions in *The Art of D. H. Lawrence* (Cambridge UP, 1966). Gerald Solomon, 'The Banal, and the Poetry of D. H. Lawrence', *Essays in Criticism* 23 (1973), offers intelligent discussion not of how critically favoured poems work, but of how other poems fail.

# INDEX TO TITLES

# INDEX OF
# FIRST LINES